THE 'one' Invisible CODE

An Uncommon **Formula** To **Breakthrough** Mediocrity & **Rise** to the **Next Level**

SHARAT SHARMA

SPOTLIGHT
by notionpress

SPOTLIGHT

No.8, 3rd Cross Street,
CIT Colony, Mylapore,
Chennai, Tamil Nadu – 600004

First Published by Notion Press 2020
Copyright © Sharat Sharma 2020
All Rights Reserved.

ISBN 978-1-64650-662-0

This book has been published with all efforts taken to make the material error-free after the consent of the author. However, the author and the publisher do not assume and hereby disclaim any liability to any party for any loss, damage, or disruption caused by errors or omissions, whether such errors or omissions result from negligence, accident, or any other cause.

While every effort has been made to avoid any mistake or omission, this publication is being sold on the condition and understanding that neither the author nor the publishers or printers would be liable in any manner to any person by reason of any mistake or omission in this publication or for any action taken or omitted to be taken or advice rendered or accepted on the basis of this work. For any defect in printing or binding the publishers will be liable only to replace the defective copy by another copy of this work then available.

Names, characters, businesses, places, events, locales, and incidents are either the products of the author's imagination or used in a fictitious manner. Any resemblance to actual persons, living or dead, or actual events is purely coincidental.

Dedicated to the Dreamer in You!

Dreamers are those who dance to the tune of a different drummer!

**When the world dictates limitations,
the dreamer refuses to accept them.**

**When the world believes it is impossible,
the dreamer stands tall and says, "Let's make it possible."**

**When the world wants to give up, the dreamer says,
"Quitting is not an option."**

PRAISES FOR THE BOOK

Sharat's approach will engage and inspire you to redefine your aspirations. The "One" Invisible Code will provide you with easy-to-consume, actionable ideas to tap into your potential and achieve exceptional results.

Marshall Goldsmith – New York Times #1 bestselling Author, #1 Executive Coach and #1 Leadership Thinker in the world.

Sharat will inspire you on a journey of self-discovery with a practical blueprint to tap your full potential. The One Invisible Code will uplift your success, in work, at home, and in life. A great read for those ready to be or become high-achievers!

Ron Kaufman, New York Times bestselling author of Uplifting Service

"This wonderful, inspiring book opens your eyes and stimulates your mind with timeless success principles and ideas."

Brian Tracy, Author, World Renowned Speaker, Top selling author of over 70 books.

Timeless wisdom, shared through the eyes of Sharat and the words by men and women of the past and present. Simply, yet powerfully packaged in the book you hold in your hands. Read it. Gift it. The lessons need to be shared.

Ankur Warikoo – Founder Nearbuy.com, Mentor, Angle Investor, Public Speaker

"This book isn't just about personal development. It is about maximizing your potential. If you are looking to achieve mastery overall, you should read Sharat's book. It's a genuine, principle-centered and a powerful motivational message you need to read right now."

Ron Malhotra International Wealth Expert, #1 Best-Selling Author, Founder of 'The Successful Male'.

"The One Invisible Code is absolutely fascinating, inspiring and thought-provoking. In this book Sharat sharma takes you on an inner journey that unfolds the formula to transform from mediocrity to mastery. It has the wisdom and insights that will help you achieve extraordinary success and continuous growth both in personal and professional life while being happy and fulfilled."

Ajaya Mishra "Awesome AJ", Success Coach & India's #1 Law of Attraction Expert, Founder of Awesome AJ Academy

"This book teaches you simple and practical steps to beat Mediocrity and Achieve Mastery in every aspect of your life. If you are committed to your next level of success, you cannot miss this book."

Amandeep Thind, International Speaker, Trainer & Author. Author Of The Book is "The Secret of Winning"

"The One Invisible Code is a must read book if you want to achieve self mastery in your life. This book is a step by step guide on how you can take charge of your life."

Hitesh R Global Motivational Speaker | Paralympic Athlete | Author |

One of the most remarkable books that you will ever read, it connects to you instantly and deeply. What I liked most about the book is how Sharat has simplified the concept of breaking through mediocrity and achieving Mastery. Read this book if you are hungry to reach the next level of professional & personal success.

Bijay Gautam - Co-Founder, WYN Studio & Host of The Inspiring Talk, Finalist for Asia's Best Podcast Award.

"A delightful read that makes you think and introspect. You have to learn, not only about how to succeed, but also how to rise up when you fail and fall. Sharat makes sure that you are inspired to take action and achieve mastery in every dimension of your life. A must-read!

Gautam Ganglani, Chief Energizing Officer – CEO, Right Selection

The best thing about Sharat is that he has personally taken up this journey. So this book is not coming from the classroom learning but from his own experience. And I guess that's what move & inspire people. Truly Inspiring work!

Karan Behl, Founder of Happiitude

"If you are dreaming big but feeling like you are stuck in a rut, get your hands on The One Invisible Code. Sharat shares interesting insights, simple tips, and practical advice to help you unlock your greatness. Read it, put those ideas into action, and discover a whole new you.

Remember, it's never too late to become the person you were meant to be."

Prakash Iyer, Best Selling Author, Speaker & Leadership Coach

Praises for the Book

"Sharat has combined timeless wisdom with inspiring storytelling, and created this powerful navigation tool for anyone on their transformation journey."

Gautam Khetrapal, Founder - LifePlugin.com

CONTENTS

A Message to the Dreamer in You! *13*

PART 1

1. Connecting the Dots 25
2. The Orbit of Mastery 36
3. The Orbit of Mediocrity 58

PART 2

4. Finding Your Roar – the Mindset 69
5. Owning the Truth 89

PART 3

6. Discovering the Invisible Code 115
7. The Aspirations – Knowing the GAPP 123
8. The Beliefs – Breaking the Boundaries 133
9. The 3Cs – the Start, the Path & the Win 156
10. The 5Ds – the Freedom 171

My Story *187*

Acknowledgement *191*

Bibliography *193*

A MESSAGE TO THE DREAMER IN YOU!

The world bows to the ones who believe in the power of their dreams.

History has been witness to the fact that dreamers change the course of the world. It was the dream of one man, Mr. Mahatma Gandhi, which made an entire nation fight for its freedom. It was the dream of Mr. Nelson Mandela, which brought the world together to fight against racial injustice and inequality. It is because of one man's dream that we humans reached the moon. The fact is every great invention that we see today was someone's belief in their dream. Every record that is set and every record that someone breaks is because they believe in the power of their dreams.

When the world dictates limitations, the dreamer refuses to accept them. When the world believes it is impossible, the dreamer challenges and says, "Let's make it possible." When the world wants to give up, the dreamer says, "Quitting is not an option."

This book is for one such dreamer in you. A dreamer who believes in the power of dreams.

To the dreamer in you who is taking the first step

You have a dream—to start a new business or take on the dream leadership role in your organization or explore new avenues to multiply your income or maybe to turn your passion into profession.

Whatever is the dream that you believe in, this book is for that dream and for the dreamer in you.

I want to congratulate you for believing in your dream and taking the leap of faith.

You are like the athlete whose dream is to win the medal and be a champion. You are ready to embark upon the journey of becoming the next champion. You have the energy, passion, and willingness to learn and take action. You are ready to invest blood and sweat to make your dreams come true. As you take your mark at the start line, all you need is the right mindset, tools, and strategies.

This book will help you develop the exact mindset, tools, and strategies you need to tap into your full potential and deliver cutting-edge results like a champion.

If you identify yourself with the dreamer who is taking the first step, I invite you to immerse yourself in this journey of self-discovery and great learning.

Commit yourself to develop the mindset, tools, and strategies illustrated in this book.

Let me tell you a story. A disciple asked his master, "How can I be more successful? What are the steps that I must keep in mind while I am on this journey of being more successful?" The master smiled and replied, "Son, there are only two important steps in everything that you do: the first and the last one." He paused for a while and continued, "By asking this question, you have taken the first step. Now stay committed and finish what you have started. That's what will make you more successful."

By choosing this book, you have taken the first step. Now it's your turn to finish the book and follow the proven mindset, tools, and strategies shared in the book. It's time to turn you into a champion.

> *There are two most important steps to succeed at anything - the first step and the last step.*

To the dreamer in you who has lost hope

Do you feel like you are stuck, overwhelmed, and/or lost? Are the voices in your head screaming hard and telling you to give up? Have doubts, fears, and judgments overpowered your belief in your dream?

You believed in your dream. Everything worked well for some time, but now, things are getting tougher. You are struggling to keep your dream alive. You have seen results in the past, but they did not last long. The current tough times have shaken your belief, and you feel this phase will last forever. You never wanted to settle for less but, with no other solution in sight, you are giving up on your dream. Well, don't!

Remember, the only religion of every dreamer is 'faith'!

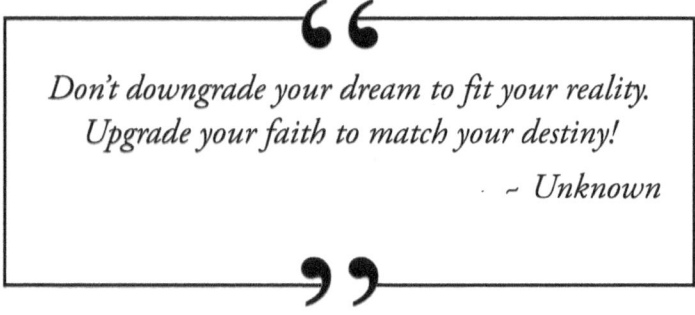

Don't downgrade your dream to fit your reality. Upgrade your faith to match your destiny!
~ Unknown

Over the past few years, I met many individuals with extraordinary potential. They have big dreams, and they also take action to turn their dreams into reality. When they do not get results, they get disheartened. Many lose hope when the results do not match their standards. They then fall into the trap of believing that their dreams will never come true. They end up settling for mediocre results or choose to give up their dreams.

Once I met a handsome and cheerful young man. His enthusiasm was infectious. After meeting him a couple of times, I discovered that he was undergoing chemotherapy. He was a teenager when he was diagnosed with life-threatening cancer. He had been fighting cancer for several years. In a conversation, he once said, "When I am on my deathbed, what will matter to me most is not whether I won or lost my fight against cancer, what will matter to me is whether I fought enough with my spirits held high." I can never forget what he said.

Even after facing a life-threatening illness, the spirit with which he was fighting and his unwillingness to give up made him a true champion.

When you experience a phase of no result or inconsistent results, and when you feel like giving up on your dream, you have three options:

The first option is to worry and give up. This is what most people choose.

The second option is to keep trying. This is what most self-help books advocate. They say when the going gets tough, the tough get going. Every time you experience a tough situation, you must persevere more.

Let me tell you a truth: perseverance without intelligence is a perfect recipe for failure.

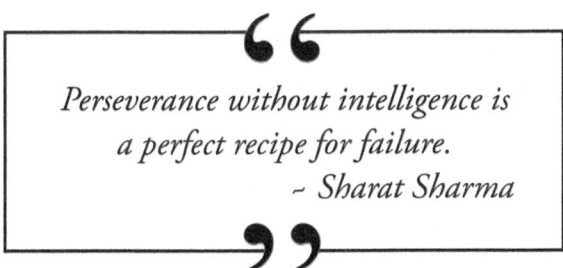

> *Perseverance without intelligence is a perfect recipe for failure.*
> ~ Sharat Sharma

Think of a time when you persevered for long and did not get results. How did you feel? Did you feel tired, upset, angered, and/or anxious? No one likes these emotions, and that is why a lot of people give up on their dreams.

If you persevere without intelligence, and if you do not have the right mindset and strategies, you will feel defeated time and again. Soon you will underplay your potential and convince yourself that you have limited potential. That's the death of your dream.

Here is the third option: whenever you fail, you learn. You be more strategic and strive harder in every next big step you take. While doing this, let your spirit be high. Be a warrior, not a worrier.

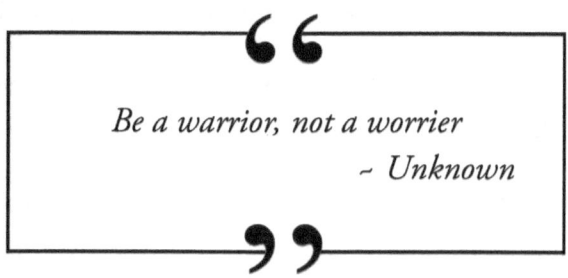

Be a warrior, not a worrier
~ Unknown

If you identify with the dreamer who has lost hope, I want you to recommit to your dreams. In this book, I am going to share with you the head, heart, and habits of fulfilling your dreams. The book deconstructs the lives of high achievers, elite athletes, global leaders, and successful entrepreneurs who once thought of giving up on their dreams just like you, but they did not.

As you read this book, you will learn an uncommon formula to breakthrough mediocrity, rekindle your inner potential, and deliver world-class results.

To the dreamer in you, who is hungry for the next level of success

In the year 2014, when I met my mentor, Mr. Les Brown, the world's leading motivational speaker, he told me, *"If you want to do anything worthwhile in your life, you got to be hungry!"*

I am reminded of these words whenever I meet a dreamer who is hungry for their next level of success.

As a dreamer, you have faced every challenge with strength and tenacity. You are the one who showed unwavering commitment to turn your dream into reality. You are hungry to learn and are open to taking the next big challenge.

You are aware that the next big challenge will need the next version of you. You strive to reinvent yourself. You understand that preparation is the key to success. You believe in meeting every opportunity with the right preparation.

I call you a 'champion' because you do not settle for less; you believe in doing whatever it takes to achieve your dreams. Unshakable faith and unbreakable commitment are the virtues of a champion!

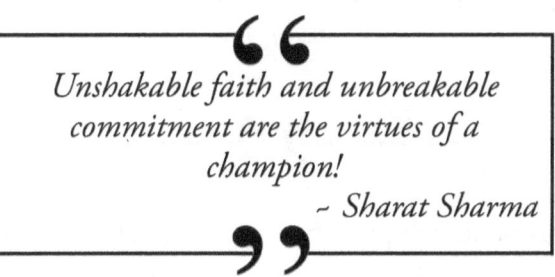

> *Unshakable faith and unbreakable commitment are the virtues of a champion!*
> ~ Sharat Sharma

Usain Bolt won nine gold medals in the last three Olympics. He ran less than two minutes (115 seconds to be precise) on the track. That's the economy of his effort! But he made a whopping 119 million dollars for this achievement. That's more than $1 million for every second he ran! That's indeed a new unit of speed for the 'run for money'.

Look at the numbers again. $1 million per second. But, for these two minutes of fame, he trained for over 15 years. Now that's the kind of investment I am talking about.

The prize money won by Bolt looks fascinating to everyone, but when you learn about the work behind the money, you will see a lot more. The kind of consistency in training, hunger, and commitment to action is commendable. These signify how much he believed in his dream and what made him a champion. Every champion I have met and studied has these traits.

If you identify with the group of dreamers who are hungry for the next level of success, I want you to know that in the pursuit of fulfilling your dream and reaching your potential, you need a high sense of self-awareness. You must break through every resistance and never settle for mediocre results. Be aware that if you sit back and relax, you will fall into the trap of getting too comfortable. Always remember that comfort is the biggest enemy of a champion.

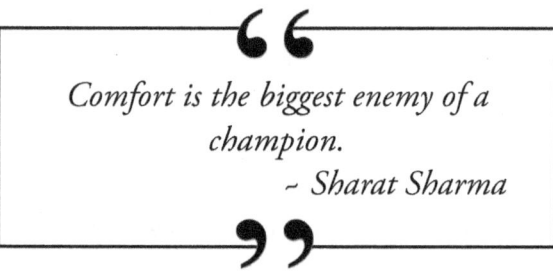

> *Comfort is the biggest enemy of a champion.*
> ~ Sharat Sharma

For you, this book will play the role of a catalyst and help you expand your self-awareness; it will help you understand the unknown resistance that might slow you down from reaching the next level of success. The book provides you with tools to build a powerful mindset and strategies that will help you reach your next level of personal and professional success.

Why did I write this book?

Let me tell you why I wrote this book. The truth is, I have always been a dreamer. There were times when I failed; every time I failed, I felt stuck and miserable. There were times when I thought of giving up my dream. But then I held onto my dreams with the belief that one day, I would turn them into reality, and I did. Even today, I continue to stay hungry, and I continue to reinvent myself.

My heart breaks every time I hear or see someone giving up their dream. I know for sure that the dream would have died, but the dreamer never dies. Every time I meet dreamers, who left their dreams half-way because they did not know how to pursue them, I can feel their pain. I know that they have let their doubts, fears, and judgments destroy their dreams. With no hope, they buried those dreams. Even though the dream has died, the dreamer in them is still alive. Even now, all they want to know is how they can turn their dream into reality.

With this book, I want to help the dreamer in you.

My intention, through this book, is to help as many dreamers as possible, including you, so that no dream would ever die.

Here is what I want you to ask before you immerse yourself in this book.

What would you do if you had only one year to live?

Anthony Burgess was 40 when he learned that he had only one year to live. He had a brain tumor that would kill him within a year. He knew that he had a battle on his hands. He was completely broke at the time, and he didn't have anything to leave behind for his wife, Lynne, who would soon become a widow.

Burgess had never been a professional novelist in the past, but he always knew he had the potential in him to be a writer. So, for the sole purpose of leaving behind royalties for his wife, he placed a sheet of paper in his typewriter and began writing. He had no certainty that his writing would even be published, but he couldn't think of anything else to do.

"It was the January of 1960," he said, "and according to the prognosis, I had a winter, spring, and summer to live through, and would die with the fall of the leaf."

During that time, Burgess wrote energetically, finishing five-and-a-half novels before the year went by (very nearly the entire lifetime output of E.M. Forster and almost twice that of J.D. Salinger).

But Burgess did not die. His cancer had gone into remission and then disappeared altogether. In his long and full life as a novelist (he is best known for A Clockwork Orange), he wrote more than 70 books, but without the death sentence, he may not have written at all.

Many of us are like Anthony Burgess, hiding our greatness inside, waiting for some external emergency to bring out our hidden potential. Ask yourself this question: If I had just a year to live, how would I live differently? What exactly would I do?

The answer to this question determines everything!

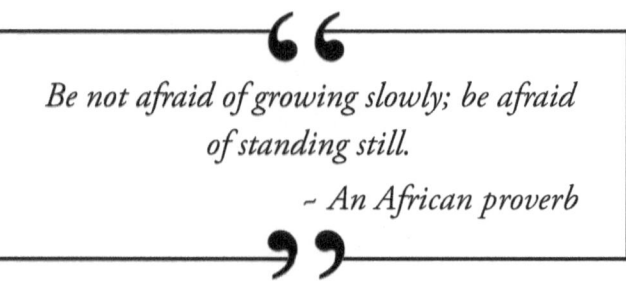

> *Be not afraid of growing slowly; be afraid of standing still.*
>
> *~ An African proverb*

PART 1

CHAPTER 1

CONNECTING THE DOTS

Steve Jobs said it right. "You cannot connect the dots looking forward; you can only connect them looking backward. You have to trust that the dots will somehow connect in your future."

As I look back at my life and connect the dots, I realize that a lot has changed in the past few years. I remember how I started my journey. I was an average student at school. My first experience with entrepreneurship was when I launched a food catering business. It was on the day of my graduation that I borrowed 100 rupees from my mother and got a few visiting cards printed. I then announced to my friends that I was starting a business. I had no clue what I was up to. I started with sheer will. Being from a traditional middle-class family, giving up education was out of scope, so I continued studying; I pursued post-graduation and also picked up orders for the catering business.

Later, I started a fast food joint and did some odd businesses, but then I gave up everything to start my corporate stint.

From setting up odd businesses and giving up most of them to taking up a corporate job, the journey has been a real roller-coaster ride.

Honestly, when I chose the corporate job, I followed what society wanted me to do. But then I always knew that I wanted to do something different. A job was never for me. And as they say, every story has three things in common: a Dream, Struggles, and Victory. My story started with the dream of being an entrepreneur and a world-class speaker. I wanted to travel around the world and inspire people. I wanted to encourage everyone to follow their dreams and help them discover their potential. However, I found myself stuck and struggling in a job that I never wanted to pursue.

After struggling for several years, finally, in the year 2013, I started my consulting business. Today, I run a successful business and live a dream life. I travel, speak at various events, and coach corporate executives and business owners. I help individuals and businesses discover their potential and also help them build a profitable business.

So, going back to what Steve Jobs said about connecting the dots, how do the dots connect in my life?

It all started when I was experiencing chaos in my life. It was early 2012 when I felt that the things I did at my job were not fueling my aspirations. My friends and relatives thought of me as someone who was highly successful and happy. They felt that I had a well-paid job, but no one knew what I was going through and how I felt. I was working as a senior leader in a large private organization. Yes, I was successful, but then I never felt fulfilled.

When I looked around, I saw most people just like me, unhappy and unfulfilled. They would wake up every morning dreading to go to work, just like me. I was one among the many with no identity of my own. I hated everything that was happening around me. I wanted to do more. I was aspiring to start my own business, create a bigger impact, and a lot more. I knew that if I did not change, my aspirations would soon die within me. But I could never gather the courage to change.

Then one day, it just happened. I was fired from my job.

It was in early November 2012. Over the past couple of weeks, I had noticed changes in the behavior of my colleagues; I wondered why. Every time I asked the reason, I only received unusual silence as a response. One day, like any other day, I reached my workplace early and kept myself busy doing my work.

At around 10:30 a.m., a senior colleague walked up to me and asked me to accompany him for some urgent discussion. The voice and the manner in which he called made me feel very uncomfortable. I could sense that something was not right. He escorted me into a meeting room, and the discussion began. By the time I could figure out what was going on, I was told that they felt that I was stealing confidential company data. I defended and said that it wasn't true. The argument continued, and I spent the most humiliating five hours of my life. I was labeled a thief without validating the facts. I was asked several questions as if I had committed a crime. I felt emotionally drained, and at the end of the day, I received a termination letter.

From being a leader in a large corporate to being no one, it all happened in the blink of an eye. It was difficult for me to even believe that it had actually happened. I felt betrayed and pained. I told myself that all the hard work and commitment did not matter to the organization and the team I was working with. I held on to the pain for too long, so long that my aspirations turned into anger, anxiety, frustration, and self-doubt. These were my only companions for a long time. And I chose to be with them.

For several weeks, everything just felt shallow and meaningless. Escaping from all the chaos was the only option that I could think of. I guess when we are not bold enough to handle the challenges life throws at us, we all try to escape. And that's exactly what I chose to do. I booked a flight just to escape from the chaos around me. Little did I know that life had different plans for me.

> *You will meet chaos and confusion on your path to clarity. Own this truth!*
> ~ Sharat Sharma

The 'One' Invisible Code

It was half-past 11 at night. I was the last one to board the flight to Himachal Pradesh, one of the mystic lands of India. As I boarded the flight, I noticed that the air hostess was not really happy to see me. It must have been because I was a few minutes late in boarding the flight. There were people from varied backgrounds in the flight—newly-married couples, middle-aged couples, newborn babies, youngsters, and elderly people. I knew it was going to be a long flight. I was tired and desperately wanted to catch some sleep. I grabbed my seat as quickly as I could. I noticed that I was sitting next to a middle-aged man. As I sat next to him, he smiled and greeted me. I did not pay much attention to him.

A few minutes after the flight took off, the plane was hit by turbulence. The turbulence was so bad that, for the first time in my life, I was scared. For a moment, I felt that this would be my last flight. I started cursing the experiences life was throwing at me. The announcement from the pilot was that the weather had turned fierce, and the turbulence could last for some more time. The pilot asked us to buckle ourselves with the seatbelt. I noticed that most passengers panicked, but the middle-aged man sitting next to me was as cool as a cucumber.

Sensing my anxiety, he smiled and said, "The pilot is making the course adjustments. He must be shifting the altitude. It's just bad weather, don't worry. Everything will be alright in a while." He then tried to pacify me by saying, "Every pilot does this to ensure that all of us have a safe flight and, more importantly, have a smooth experience."

He probably thought it was my first flight.

Just a few months ago, I was hopping from one flight to another, and I had never been scared of turbulence. Then I thought maybe it's the bad times that make one appear more fearful.

Initially, I had tried avoiding any conversation with the man. I had ignored him, as I wanted to spend time alone. Well, that was the intention behind this journey, wasn't it? But then there was something about him that was intriguing. His positive demeanor, his voice, and the peace on his face did not let me ignore him for too long. His aura, tone of voice, friendliness, and his ability to bring about a positive emphasis even during tough times were impressive. Within a few minutes of my conversation with him, I was amazed by his wisdom.

He started sharing some of the lessons he had learned in his lifetime. He had a unique way of sharing his experiences; thought-provoking stories, questions, and anecdotes laced with a lot of humor were all part of the conversation that followed. Gradually, all my resistance vanished. I was ready to listen to everything that the man had to say.

Little did I know that this meeting with the wise man would introduce me to a world of possibilities and life-changing lessons. It is said that every lesson comes to us at the right time, and if we are willing to learn the lesson and act on it, our life changes forever. Such moments are life-defining moments, and for me, this was one such moment.

The more wisdom he shared, the more comfortable I felt. I usually never feel comfortable sharing anything with a stranger, but this man was different. I did not hesitate to call him 'Master'. He had every quality a great master would have.

I shared with him how I started working at a very young age, how I was doing odd businesses like selling firecrackers, operating a food catering business, and running a fast food center. I also told him about my work in multinational companies and how I grew into a senior leader in an organization.

"After all this, I feel lost, anxious, upset, unfulfilled, stuck, and uninspired to do anything. In addition, the recent event of being terminated has left me clueless about the direction in which my life is headed," I confessed to Master.

Master smiled and said, "Every 'mess' we experience has a 'mess'age! It changes our lives only if we are willing to listen and learn from the message."

Every MESS you experience has a MESSage!
It changes our lives if we are willing to listen
and learn from the message.

Master then asked me, "Joy, did you notice what the pilot did when the flight was experiencing turbulence?"

I replied, "As you said, he was adjusting the course or changing the altitude."

Master said, "Our lives are the same. When we experience challenges, all we need to do is adjust our course by changing. Do you know what happens if the pilot does not make the course adjustment, Joy?"

I replied, "The plane crashes!"

Master said, "Not really; the plane is powerful enough to withstand the rough weather. We may not crash immediately, but eventually, we will, only if we do not adjust the course. But at first, we will not have a smooth experience; it might feel like the end.

That's what happens in our lives too. We all are powerful enough to withstand every challenge that life throws at us. All we must do is adjust the course by changing when the time is right."

I asked, "If this is so simple, why don't people do it?"

"It is simple. But most people want to do the thing that makes them feel safe and not the things that are simple. In fact, if you notice, every time you face a challenging situation, there is a voice in your head that screams and tells you things like, 'Don't do it now, it must be hard', 'It's not that urgent', 'This is not the best time', 'It's too much effort now; why take all the effort?'

When there is a challenging situation, we can think rationally and confront the challenge, or we can avoid and escape from facing the challenge. Thinking rationally and overcoming the challenge is simple, but we listen to the voices in our head and assume that avoiding and escaping is safe"

Master was telling me exactly what I was doing. I was escaping, and this was because I never wanted to confront the challenges, and it felt safe to just escape. But is that the right thing to do? I asked myself.

I then asked Master, "What if avoiding and escaping is the only thing that feels safe?"

"Joy, when you escape or do the thing that does not allow you to grow, it is just an illusion of safety. When you want to feel safe, all you want is to avoid the risk of failing, but then let's think for a moment. What is the biggest risk? The biggest risk in life is not failing; it is not making progress and staying stuck. It is not living up to one's own potential and not doing the things that matter the most. The biggest risk is taking all your aspirations to your deathbed."

That was deep and made me think about what regrets I would face if I continued to escape.

Master then continued, "Most people want to escape because they are unwilling or uncomfortable to change. A lot of times, even if they are unhappy and are suffering, they are reluctant to change. They fail to understand that the only thing which can make them happy is taking action in the right direction. In simple terms, it is to make progress.

While some people do not take the right action in the right direction, others deceive themselves with actions that are insignificant. Things, like being glued to technology, gossiping about problems, and being addicted to unhealthy habits, are actions that cause deception in the mind."

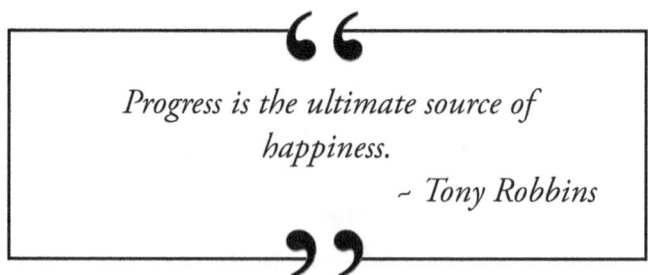

Progress is the ultimate source of happiness.
~ Tony Robbins

"Master, tell me a little more about how people deceive themselves?"

"Joy, the truth is, if one has to change, they have to take action. However, some people over-anticipate the future and feel uncertain and fearful, while others live in their past and feel safe and secure. Both of this stops them from taking the right action in the present. Postponing actions, over-anticipation, and trying to perfect everything are all mechanisms we adopt to deceive ourselves from changing."

"I understand this now, Master."

"Joy, the truth is, your past has nothing to do with your future. But your present has everything to do with your future. If you want to rise to the next level in your personal and professional life, you cannot escape from taking the next step in the present."

"Master, every time I want to take the next step, I am filled with the anticipation of results. Like you rightly said, I get stuck because I am constantly anticipating the future. I want to know if anticipation is good."

"Anticipation has the power to make us or break us. When you are anticipating and willing to take the next step in the present, it will make you. But if you think there will be the best time or the best day to take action, it will break you. Stay focused on the future and take action in the present. That's the key.

Remember, like how the flight made course adjustment immediately when it faced turbulence, you must make changes immediately when you face challenges. When you take action to change, it will help you grow both personally as well as professionally."

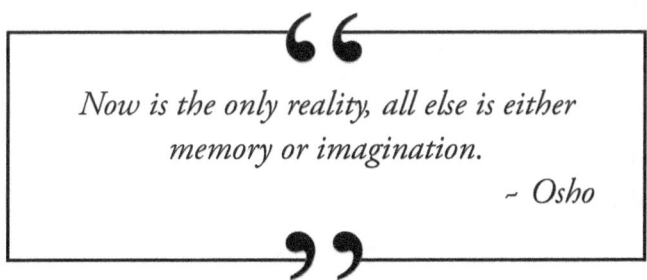

> *Now is the only reality, all else is either memory or imagination.*
> ~ Osho

I felt as if Master was reading my mind. He was telling me everything that I had to understand. Deep inside, I knew I was escaping. I was escaping from taking the next step. I had no courage to change, and now Master had just shown me the mirror. The truth!

I asked Master, "So, how does one adjust their course in life? What are the things that I must do to change? At this point in my life, I realize that I am escaping and avoiding change. I wish to start a new journey, but I have had a bitter past, and I have no clue what the future has in store for me. You can clearly see that I am quite overwhelmed. I agree that my past has nothing to do with my future, and my present is all that I have. So, how should I change and adjust the course of my journey? What are the things that I must do 'now' so that I can craft a better future for myself?"

I flooded Master with all the questions I had in my mind. It was as if he was the genie who had risen from the lamp; he had all the answers to my questions, and I had been waiting for him to appear in front of me all my life. I was reminded of the old saying, "When the student is ready, the teacher appears." Master had all the wisdom. I had all the thirst and eagerness to listen and learn. I felt I was ready and willing to learn.

After some time, Master said, "Remember Joy, the world is constantly influencing and feeding information that is irrelevant and mostly disempowering. It tells you all the things that are wrong with you than telling you things that are amazing in you. It tells you what you should think and what you should not think, what you must do and what you must not do. It dictates rules on you. Most of these rules advocate ***safety over growth, comfort over challenge, and short-term pleasure over long-term purpose.*** It wants you to play small and remain mediocre."

"So, Master, how should I break through this mediocrity?"

Master sipped some coffee from his mug and looked out of the window. Both of us were quiet for a while. All I could see were stars twinkling in the midst of the dark sky. It made the sky appear beautiful. At this moment, my life was like the dark sky, and this conversation gave me a ray of hope.

Then Master looked at me and said, "Success in life or in business is all about bridging the gap between your potential and your current results.

To break through mediocrity, you must constantly tap into your potential and challenge your current results. To tap into your innate potential and challenge your current results, you must consciously practice being in the 'orbit of mastery'."

I nodded, affirming my belief in him and expressing my inquisitiveness to know more. I was eager to learn more about the orbit of mastery.

CHAPTER 2

THE ORBIT OF MASTERY

> *In a world where limitations are discussed over possibilities, mastery is the path chosen by only a few.*
> ~ Sharat Sharma

"Joy, do you know why only a few people live up to their full potential? What makes a few choose the path of mastery? Why do many people never realize their full potential?" Master enquired.

My silence only meant that I had no answer.

Master said, "It is because they lack self-awareness!"

Master then explained, "To live up to your potential, you must constantly work on expanding your self-awareness. All high achievers, elite athletes, global leaders, and successful entrepreneurs constantly work on expanding their self-awareness. They know that their results expand or shrink in proportion to their self-awareness.

When you lack self-awareness or when you are ignorant, you are likely to get influenced by everything and everyone around you. Other people's lives appeal to you more than your faith in your potential. As a result, you get distracted by external sources, and you stop relying on your internal powers. You look for solutions outside of you, while the truth is, every solution that you are searching for is within you. This lack of self-awareness results in mediocre results."

Master continued, "Joy, when you are hooked to all the distractions around you, you are unaware of the fact that these distractions are only causing destructions within you. These distractions influence your thoughts, feelings, beliefs, and decisions. They destroy your self-image and distort your perception. All of these create friction between your potential and the current results. This friction eventually slows you down."

"Master, I want to know where do these influences come from, and how do they influence me?"

Master answered patiently, "These influences come from your environment. The truth is, your environment is constantly shaping your thoughts, feelings, beliefs, and decisions. That's why it is said that your current environment is a perfect indicator of how your life is going to shape up in the future.

Many of these influences started with people who played a significant role and those who are an authority in your life. They could be someone from the family or society or peers you grew up with. It is also from the books you read, the television shows you watch and a lot more. Most of these influences come in the form of values, beliefs, and rules that you were expected to follow. If you did not follow any of these, you were judged and questioned. The fear of being judged and questioned made you conform to everyone around you. The more you conformed, the more it slowed you down from exploring your potential. This is how other people's limitations became your limitations, and they continued to influence and control your life. All of these led you to live a mediocre life."

I asked, "How long does this continue?"

Master, "This will continue until the day you take a pause and become aware of these influences and then break these influences. Let me share with you an experiment that was done."

The 'One' Invisible Code

A scientist puts five monkeys in a large cage. High up, at the top of the cage, well beyond the reach of the monkeys, is a bunch of bananas. Underneath the bananas is a ladder. The monkeys immediately spot the bananas, and one of them begins to climb the ladder. As he climbs up, the scientist sprays him with a stream of cold water. Then he proceeds to spray the other monkeys.

The monkey on the ladder scrambles down. All the monkeys sit for some time on the floor, wet, cold, and bewildered. Soon the temptation of the bananas gets to them. Another monkey begins to climb the ladder. Again, the scientist sprays the ambitious monkey and all the other monkeys with cold water. When a third monkey tries to climb up the ladder, the other monkeys, wanting to avoid the cold spray, pull him off the ladder and beat him.

Now the scientist removes one monkey, and a new monkey is introduced into the cage. Spotting the bananas, the new monkey naively begins to climb up the ladder. The other monkeys pull him off the ladder and beat him.

Here's where it gets interesting. The scientist removes another monkey from the original group and replaces him with another new monkey. Again, the new monkey begins to climb up the ladder. Again, the other monkeys pulled him off and beat him, including the monkey, who has not been sprayed.

Master then explained, "Most of us are like the monkeys. We got beaten up every time we tried. And soon, we learned not to try."

Every word Master said resonated with me. I was like the monkey in the experiment who wanted to do more but then eventually had to slow down because people around me discouraged me from being myself. Whenever I tried something different and failed, they laughed at me but never came forward to help. I realized that my current environment was not supportive.

"Joy, all these influences eventually turn into your limiting beliefs. You now find yourself fighting a battle between your limiting beliefs and your unlimited potential. This makes you experience a lot of chaos inside your mind. This chaos turns into reactive behavior. As a result of these limiting beliefs, you experience only a limited part of your potential. This leads you to live a life of mediocrity, which is filled with fear, anger, anxiety, self-doubt, frustration, judgments, and assumptions."

"These are the exact emotions that I am feeling right now."

The fact is, when you are too caught in these influences, you are not even aware of what is causing the chaos in your life. You believe that things cannot change. Most of the time, you do not even realize that all of this is leading you to the path of mediocrity.

The challenge with being influenced by others' beliefs is that you give your power away to others. You become a mere puppet in the hands of others. You complain, criticize, and condemn more than accepting full responsibility for your life.

"So, how does one seek mastery and not mediocrity?"

"A life of mastery happens when you tune inward and accept full responsibility for your life. As you tune inward, you look within and seek clarity. This clarity brings about responsive behavior. You gain clarity by becoming aware of your current values, beliefs, thoughts, and feelings and how they are shaping your life. The more you become aware, the more you realize that some of your values, beliefs, thoughts, and feelings are not serving you in your growth and are limiting your potential. The more you understand and accept responsibility of your life, the more you know that you hold the power to change the course of your life by challenging these values, beliefs, thoughts, and feelings. The more you do this, the more you start unleashing your potential."

"This is brilliant, Master! So, the first step to attain mastery is awareness. I get it now."

"As you take the first step to attain mastery and expand your awareness, you start believing in your potential. You don't give in to outer influences. You don't give your power away; instead, you start exercising your power. You continue to renew your values, beliefs, thoughts, and feelings and align them with your aspirations. As you become aware of who you really are, who you are not, and who you can become, you learn to reinvent yourself constantly. This awareness facilitates the process of discovering your full potential. You are now driven by the choices that this awareness presents you."

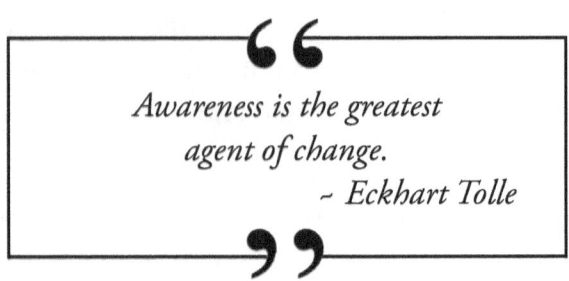

Master then shared a story.

One day, a disciple approached his guru and said, "Guruji, I came to this ashram in a quest to find answers, but I am disheartened. Before I came here, I even visited many temples and holy places, yet I could not find it. I am very disappointed. I think it's time for me to take leave of you."

Instead of responding to the disciple, the guru immediately bent down and started searching for something. The curious disciple asked, "What are you searching for, Guruji? May I help you find it?"

"Son, I lost my needle, and I am looking for it," said the guru.

The disciple joined him and began to search. After searching for a while, he humbly asked, "Do you recall where exactly you dropped it, Guruji?"

"Yes, of course. I dropped it in my hut," said the guru.

Puzzled, the disciple stood up and said, "Guruji, if you dropped it in your hut, why are we searching for it in the yard?"

"Oh, that's because it's dark inside, and I don't have any oil left to light the lamp. There is so much bright light out here, so I thought I would search here," said the guru calmly.

It immediately dawned on the disciple that what he was seeking outside was what he had lost within.

As Master completed the story, I was quiet. I started to introspect. All along my life, I had been looking for solutions outside of me. I was influenced by all the glitter of gold in society. I tried to fix things outside me and was expecting great results. While doing all of this, I allowed all the external influences to impact me negatively. I was like many others who are unaware, unwilling to change, and who stay mediocre. I realized that many beliefs that I thought were mine were actually given to me by others. Most of my life, I had been influenced by the people around me. I had been living a life that was not designed by me but was designed for me by others. This was the reason why I was not fulfilled. Now, it was my responsibility to constantly expand my level of awareness and lead myself on the path of mastery.

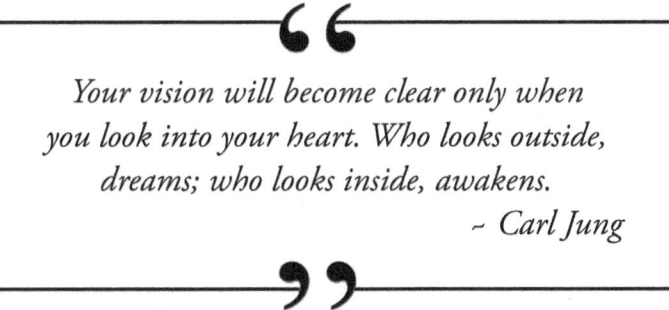

> *Your vision will become clear only when you look into your heart. Who looks outside, dreams; who looks inside, awakens.*
> ~ *Carl Jung*

Insight

As you take the path of mastery, become aware of what is happening within you, which is your inner world. It is dictated by the values, beliefs, thoughts, and feelings that you currently hold true. Also, be aware of how your inner world is shaping the world outside you. Be aware of your present; know that you have a choice, and you hold the power to change anything at this very moment.

Don't look back in life and be angry; don't look too far into the future and be fearful. Just be in the moment and be aware of everything that's happening within you and around you. Believe that you hold the greatest power to turn your potential into results and rise from mediocrity to mastery.

Remember, mastery is your journey within.

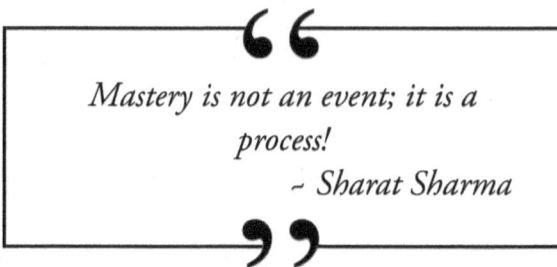

> "
> *Mastery is not an event; it is a process!*
> ~ Sharat Sharma
> "

Exercises to enhance your awareness

- Identify the areas in your life where you find yourself stuck.
- Identify the beliefs that are causing resistance and slowing you down.
- Find out if these beliefs are yours or if they were given to you by others.
- Identify the actions that you are willing to carry out to challenge these beliefs.
- Identify what being unaware has cost you in your life.

Seven ways to practice and expand self-awareness;

- Monitor your inner dialogue.
- Identify and challenge your beliefs.
- Identify and assess your core values.
- Practice everyday journaling.
- Practice meditation.
- Know your strengths and weaknesses.
- Find a coach.

Note: We will discuss how to expand your awareness and how to challenge your beliefs in the coming chapters.

Accept

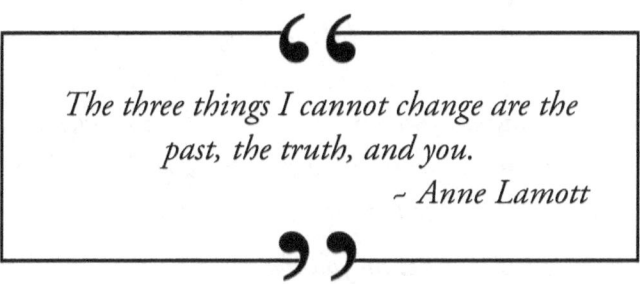

The three things I cannot change are the past, the truth, and you.
~ Anne Lamott

I noticed that most people were asleep, and the lights of the plane were dimmed. Only our light was on. The air hostess came up to us to check if we needed something. Master ordered another cup of coffee, and I ordered some water. I was just grateful that I was spending time with Master.

I was excited and inquisitive to know more. In my excitement, I said, "As one becomes aware of what is happening in the inner world and outer world, one must be willing to take the right action. Am I right?"

"Not really, Joy! If being aware is the first step to mastery, the second step is to accept what is and what is not. Acceptance is when you choose to see every experience of yours as a gift, including the experiences that were bitter. Let me tell you a story to help you understand."

A mouse was in constant distress because of his fear of the cat. He did not go out and look for his favorite food, cheese. He starved each day with the fear of being chased by the cat to death, without realizing he was nearing his death anyway. The mouse prayed for a miracle. Then one day, a magician took pity on the mouse and asked him how he could help. The mouse said, "Why don't you turn me into a cat? Then I can be free."

With his magic wand, the magician turned the mouse into a big cat. The cat was happy and free. After a few days, he became afraid of the dog. The cat prayed again, and the magician took pity again. This time, the cat asked the magician to turn him into a dog. The cat was now a ferocious dog.

As time passed, the dog started loving his life. He was loved by all; everyone gave him great food and treated him with a lot of care. One day, the dog overheard people talking about a ferocious panther in the town. The dog feared the panther and stopped eating. He did not enjoy the love of the people anymore and lived in constant worry. Now, every day, the dog dreamed of being eaten by the panther. The constant fear reminded him of the magician again, and he started searching for the magician. One day, the dog found the magician and said to him, "I heard about the panther in town, and I fear the panther."

The magician asked, "What do you want?" The dog said, "I think I want to be a panther. Being a panther will make me the best and fastest animal around, and I can surely be fearless." The magician was upset, but he turned the dog into a panther.

The panther was fearless and enjoyed his speed. Soon, he realized that the people who cared for him as a dog and gave him food did not visit him. Instead, they feared him the most. The friends he had made as a dog had now become his hunters. He ran into the jungle, away from all the people who once loved him and surrounded him. Every day, the panther feared being hunted by the humans.

The panther felt lonely and started to pray for the magician. Then the magician appeared before him and asked him what he truly wanted. But without listening to the panther, the magician turned him into a mouse saying, "Nothing I do for you is ever going to help you because you always want to be something more. You always want to be someone else; you always feel incomplete with your own self. The thing that you fear is not outside of you, but it is within you. Though you were a cat, a dog, and a panther, you always had the heart of a mouse. You cannot be anything else but a mouse. Accept yourself; that's the only true thing."

As Master ended the story, I took a deep breath and said, "First, we lack awareness and stay ignorant of our potential. We then constantly believe that we lack something. We assume that to be accepted by others, we need to be like someone else, be something else or do something more. We believe that's the only way we can succeed and achieve mastery. What we do not realize is that we fall into a trap—a trap of rejecting ourselves. In all of this, we become everything that others want us to become and not what we are capable of becoming. To feel accepted by others, we reject ourselves. That's why the next most important thing is to accept who we are!"

Master said, "I am glad that you understand this, Joy. In the contest of being something else, someone else, and something more, you end up losing your authentic self. You start to live a lie. You accept others' beliefs, values, and rules to feel accepted by others. Soon you develop low self-esteem. Many a time, you succeed but then you are unhappy with yourself because you have accepted others, but unknowingly you have rejected yourself. This never-ending battle of non-acceptance and trying to fit into society leads you to the path of mediocrity and not mastery."

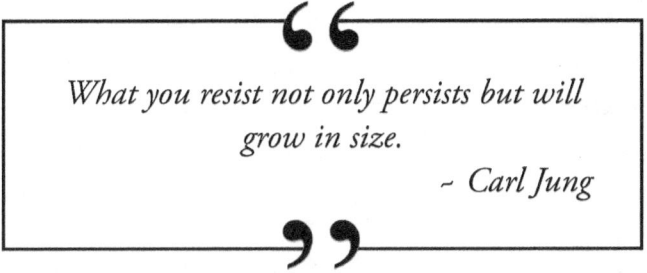

What you resist not only persists but will grow in size.
~ Carl Jung

Master continued, "The fact is that the battle of acceptance is an inside job. The more we try to fill the so-called void with external influence, the more we lose our authentic self. It is like filling a bottomless pit. You may solve one problem, but soon another one shows up, and the cycle continues forever."

I asked, "When we are open to accepting ourselves fully, should we also accept our flaws? Don't we become vulnerable?"

"When you start accepting yourself, you become more authentic to who you are. Yes, when you are open to accepting your flaws, you become

The 'One' Invisible Code

vulnerable, but this vulnerability helps you reach your potential. Often, when you discover things about yourself that do not empower you, you have two choices: accept and change them, or accept, let go, and move on. In both cases, you only grow.

When you are aware of who you truly are, when you accept to live an authentic and congruent life, you convert every obstacle into an opportunity, fear into faith, and resistance into acceleration."

Master said after a brief pause, "For a moment, let us shift our focus and do some reflection. What if you actually do not lack anything, and all you need to do is accept yourself completely? My question is, who would you become with complete acceptance?"

I was silent as I pondered over the question.

"Joy, when you operate from the feeling of 'I lack something', you not only affect yourself, but you also affect how other people treat you. Accept yourself, embrace yourself! That's the most empowering choice you can ever make. Be aware that every time you become busy rejecting and judging yourself, you only get trapped in your limitations. But the moment you choose to accept yourself, you set yourself free. As you do, you get introduced to the unlimited potential within you. A lot of people reject themselves; that's why they live an unfulfilled life."

The process of becoming who you will be begins first with the total acceptance of who you are.
~ Henepola Gunaratana

Master had actually shaken my core belief. All my life, I had been unwilling to accept my flaws and pretended to be strong. In fact, I remembered how I always pretended that I knew it all, just so that I could be accepted by those around me. I feared rejection from others and did not realize that in the process, I was rejecting my own self. I was scared of being seen as someone incapable or not knowledgeable enough. I chose to pretend and enjoyed wearing a mask. I could now see how by completely accepting myself, I can reach my full potential. Also, when I identify my flaws, I have the choice to accept and change or accept, let go, and move on.

***

INSIGHT

As you take the path of mastery, be willing to accept who you truly are and who you are not. Be aware that when you are willing to accept your true self, *you hold the power to change* everything at that *very moment. Don't look around and try to fit in. Do not try to become someone you are not. Do not seek external validation. Do not accept everything that others tell you. Do not reject who you truly are. Accept and be congruent with who you truly are.*

Being authentic is the greatest gift you can give yourself. Accept yourself, embrace yourself!

> *Acceptance of facts is a pre-condition to action. Non-acceptance is an ideal condition for the reaction.*

Exercises to enhance your acceptance

- Identify the things about you that you are not accepting.
- Identify the areas of your life in which, in order to be accepted by others, you were rejecting your own self.
- Identify what this rejection or non-acceptance has cost you.

Seven ways to practice self-acceptance and increase your self-esteem

- Embrace your imperfections.
- Stop self-criticism and practice self-compassion.
- Shield yourself from others' criticism and practice self-appreciation.
- Confront your fears.
- Stop being in the comparison trap.
- Build your self-worth.
- Count your accomplishments.

Action

Our flight was cruising at 35,000 feet above sea level. I had boarded the flight thinking of catching some sleep, but this conversation had taken me one step closer to fulfilling my dreams. I was unable to sleep, and I was introspecting on the insights that Master had shared with me. There was a silence in the flight, and there was silence within me. I couldn't remember the last time I had experienced such silence. I remembered the famous quote of Dr A.P.J. Abdul Kalam. He once said, "Dream is not the thing you see in sleep but is that thing that doesn't let you sleep."

Master said, "When you are aware of your inner world and are open to accepting yourself fully, you know what you can change and what you cannot. You have now crossed half the distance in your journey of mastery. Here is a fact. When you are aware of your values, beliefs, rules, and are willing to accept your vulnerabilities, you are introduced to your inner potential. You are now set to conquer the infinite outer possibilities, the possibilities of taking your personal and professional success to the next level.

The only way to bridge your inner potential with greater outer possibilities is by taking action, and that's the next step. The more actions you take, the more you alter your current results. A lot of times, we choose not to take action, or we get paralyzed while taking action because of the relationship we have with the process of taking action. Many of us associate a lot of pain with taking action and hence choose inaction, hesitation, or procrastination."

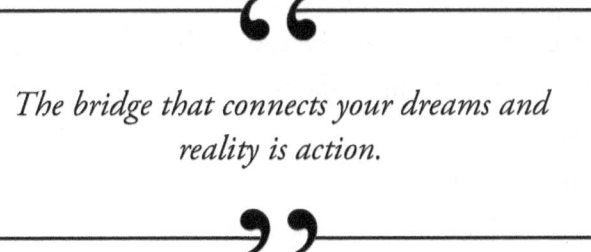

The bridge that connects your dreams and reality is action.

Master then pulled out a notepad and started drawing four quadrants. Pointing to the diagram, he said, "Let us evaluate our relationship with pain."

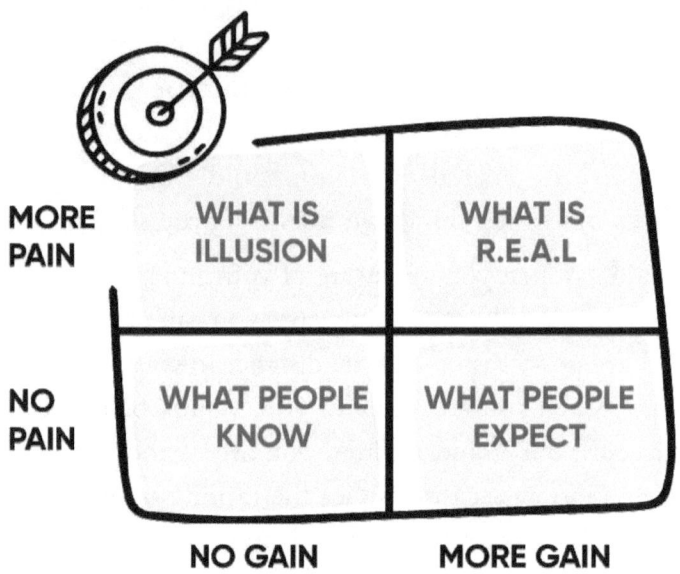

The quadrant of limited knowing: Most people know that there is no gain without any pain. But this is not the complete truth; it is only a half-truth that most people buy into. The fact of knowing that there is no gain without pain alone doesn't bring out the best in you. This is because we do not really know what pain we are capable of enduring. Being in this quadrant does not let you stretch and experience the potential you hold.

The quadrant of false expectation: What some people want is more gain with little or no pain. They hold onto this false expectation. This is like wanting to enjoy the view from the top of the mountain but unwilling to even take the first step to climb the mountain. This false expectation only leads to disappointment and then inaction. You eventually give up.

The quadrant of illusion: One of the fascinating things about humans is that they assume a lot and build their life on these assumptions. Most of these assumptions are just illusions, which limit them. One such illusion is that there may not be much gain even after enduring all the pain. Remember, this is just an illusion and not a reality; this is a myth that stops you from taking action.

The quadrant of reality: The reality is that the more pain you are willing to endure, the more gain you will experience. This is the complete truth. Every champion you meet will tell you that pain is a powerful driving force, be it mental or physical. A muscle only grows while you go through pain. You can avoid pain and let it destroy you or endure the pain and let it guide you. You can choose to go through pain, or you can decide to grow through pain.

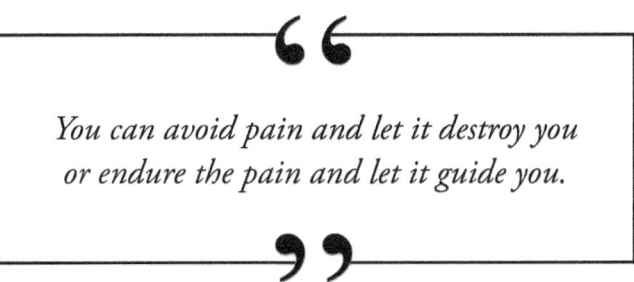

You can avoid pain and let it destroy you or endure the pain and let it guide you.

All the great achievers know this truth. They are willing to endure the pain. Take, for example, Michael Jordan. He attributes his success to all the failures and pain he endured. He has claimed that pain has made him try even harder.

Master then summarized, "Most people stay in the first three quadrants, but those who are seeking mastery are always willing to endure all the pain. They know that more pain leads to more gain, and it is pain that gives birth to a new life. This is the truth that most people fail to understand. Do not let pain destroy you; let it drive you towards your victory."

I was awestruck with what Master had just shared. I was probably in every other quadrant than the quadrant of reality.

Master continued, "Every result that you experience in your personal and professional life, or every progress that you make is a direct reflection of three aspects—your level of awareness, your ability to accept yourself and your vulnerabilities, and most importantly your willingness to take action.

When you are consistent in your actions, it further expands your awareness, deepens your strengths, and exposes you to many more vulnerabilities. It reveals to you your authentic self and your full potential.

Joy, what will you do when your actions fail?"

"If my actions fail, I must try again?"

"Correct, Joy. If your actions fail, it means you must change your actions, and it does not mean you should stop taking actions. Most people choose the latter, and they stop taking action. If the action does not work, you must try again, but this time with more awareness. Otherwise, you will repeat the same mistake over and over again. Then you end up convincing yourself that your potential is limited. You may then get disheartened and eventually give up.

While most people stop after facing failure and remain mediocre, you must take every failure as feedback and expand your awareness. The same is true with actions that give you results; they must help you expand your awareness. It is the lack of action or inconsistency in taking action that introduces you to doubts, fears, and guilt. They shrink your awareness further and take you on the path of mediocrity. In simple words, your awareness expands and shrinks in proportion to the action you take and the feedback you are willing to accept."

Master then gave me this life-changing advice. "Joy, those who do not take action fail to understand the fact that nothing is void or empty in our lives."

In the absence of faith, doubt takes the space.
In the absence of love, hate takes the space.
In the absence of discipline, excuses take the space.
In the absence of a plan, confusion takes the space.
In the absence of action, fear takes the space.

"As Mahatma Gandhi once said, 'Your action always expresses your priorities.' So, set your priorities right and take action!" concluded Master.

I had always known that inaction or lack of consistent action was causing me a lot of pain. But I had never realized that I had to work on my relationship with pain. Now I understood that I had always been dancing between the quadrants of illusion and false expectation. I had never been ready to face the reality that the more pain I endured, the more gain I would find in my journey towards mastery.

INSIGHT

As you take the path of mastery, choose to act. Know that you alone have the power to take action. Don't wait for the ideal time to act. Do not wait for things to be perfect. Never wait for the world to agree with your action and then decide to act. Know what relationship you have with pain and just act!

Remember, there is never a replacement for consistent and committed action.

Exercises to enhance your ability to act

- ❖ Identify the areas of your life where you are not taking action.
- ❖ Find out your relationship with pain.
- ❖ Identify the quadrant(s) you see yourself in.
- ❖ Find out what inaction has cost you so far in life.

Five ways to practice taking action

- ❖ Practice prioritizing important actions.
- ❖ Practice being more resilient.
- ❖ Identify and avoid distractions.
- ❖ Find an accountability partner.
- ❖ Reward taking action.

Accelerate

I was immersed in every word Master was speaking. I was keen to know what else was going to unfold to keep me in the orbit of mastery. Master looked at his watch and asked me whether I wanted to catch some sleep. I said, "No," as I wanted to make the most of my time with Master.

"Joy, have you ever heard about escape velocity?"

I replied based on what I vividly remembered from my school days, "It is the velocity needed to escape gravitational pull."

"You are right! As you start taking action and start experiencing results, you too will need escape velocity."

"What do you mean, Master?" I exclaimed.

"When you take the journey into mastery, you will experience maximum resistance and hesitation in the initial phase. This resistance and hesitation will act as the forces that slow you down. There will be times when the option of settling for the results that you have got will seem the most appealing to you. There will be times when the voices in your head will ask you to stop trying harder. People around you will tell you that the results you have got are enough. However, if you choose to take consistent and committed action, which is the foundation of building momentum, you will break through all hesitation and also escape from all the resistance. The more consistent action you take, the sooner you accelerate into achieving mastery. That's the next and final step in the orbit of mastery. As you accelerate and build momentum, you learn to be your best.

If you fail to accelerate, you will fall back into the trap of mediocrity. The path of mastery is less crowded than the oft-treaded route. All resistance and hesitation that you encounter fades away on this path. This happens only when you choose to never settle for what you get and continue to accelerate to the next level. Remember this, Joy, wherever you are, in everything that you do, there is always a next level waiting for you to be achieved."

This was an *AHA* moment!

When I look back at my life, I realize that I always settled for what I got and never believed that there could be another level possible for me. I did not consciously pursue the next level. Every time I took action and got results, I just assumed that if anything better was possible, I would have achieved it. I never accelerated or built momentum. The thoughts that Master shared made me think about how I must constantly strive to expand my awareness and be willing to accept myself completely. This would enable me to take consistent, committed action, and accelerate into the orbit of mastery.

INSIGHT

As you take the path of mastery, do not settle for what you have got. Step forward and accelerate into the unexplored realms. These could give you opportunities that you thought were impossible. Be willing to give up what you have to achieve what you can. The power to make that choice is with you. It's time to step up and accelerate into the world of possibilities.

It's time to accelerate!

Exercises to enhance your ability to accelerate

- ❖ Identify the areas of your life in which you have become too comfortable with the results you have achieved.
- ❖ Identify the areas of your life in which you want to build momentum.
- ❖ Identify where you want to beat your best results.
- ❖ Find out what not accelerating has cost you so far.

Five ways to practice acceleration and building momentum

- ❖ Practice being consistent.
- ❖ Leverage and learn from results.
- ❖ Practice habits that support your aspirations.
- ❖ Practice taking risks and overcoming resistance.
- ❖ Always aim to achieve the next benchmark.

ORBIT OF MASTERY

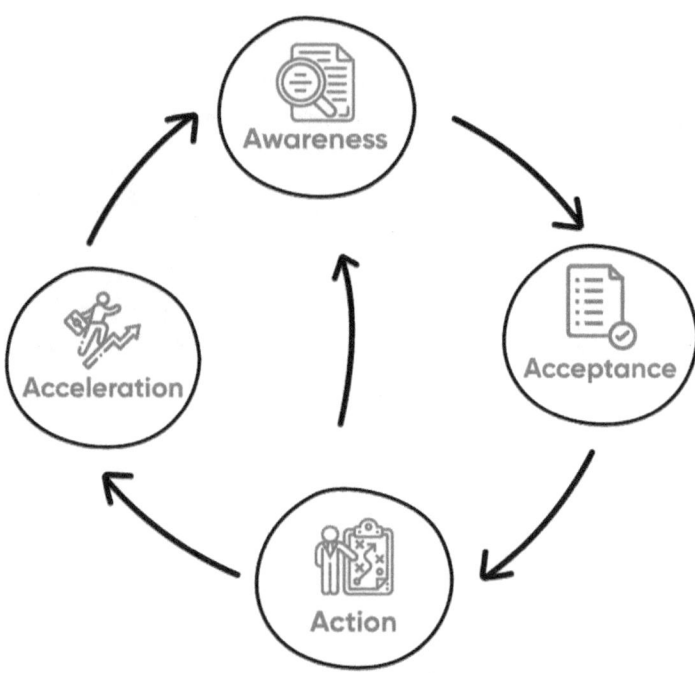

I felt as if I had received the key to a precious treasure—*the orbit of mastery*. I was overwhelmed with all that I had learned from Master.

The announcement came from the captain that the flight was ready to land. The journey that I thought would be long felt short. I was excited about embarking upon a new beginning with the treasure that I had found. Finding my master on this journey was a great blessing, indeed.

I decided that I would practice being in the orbit of mastery every day for the rest of my life. Though I was thrilled, I still felt incomplete and wanted to learn more.

Master then said softly, "The journey into the orbit of mastery is not a one-time activity but a lifetime commitment. Make sure you stay committed to this journey; otherwise, you will be dragged into the orbit of mediocrity."

As the flight touched down, everyone got ready to deplane.

I wanted to learn more. During the initial minutes of our conversation, I remembered that Master had mentioned the place he stayed in—Himachal Pradesh. He had also mentioned that, over the past few years, many people like me had visited him in search of answers and wisdom.

With a lot of hesitation, I asked him, "Master, can I visit you to seek your guidance and learn more?"

"My doors are always open for you, Joy!"

Without any second thoughts, I decided to join Master.

CHAPTER 3

THE ORBIT OF MEDIOCRITY

As we reached Master's house, we were welcomed by several people, probably his students. From their demeanor and body language, it was evident that they were very happy in the presence of Master.

Master said, "Joy, you have had a long journey; you must be tired. Take some rest, and I will see you tomorrow." He wished me a good night and walked into his room.

I was excited, and that was probably the reason I didn't feel sleepy. So, I decided to take a short walk. As I walked around the house, I was hypnotized by the beauty of the house. Everything about the house and its surroundings was magical. The house was next to a serene pond and was surrounded by greenery all around. I was grateful to Master for allowing me to stay in his house and letting me learn from him.

***

I woke up the next day curious and eager to know what would unfold in the next few days. Most people were up early, and I guess I was the last one to reach the breakfast table.

I met many interesting people over breakfast. There were people from varied backgrounds—doctors, entrepreneurs, working professionals, and others. I saw Master and greeted him. He inquired about my comfort and later told me to meet him in one of his rooms. I made a mental note of the place.

I reached the room that Master had mentioned. It looked like a library. It was Master's study room. I started asking all the questions I had in my mind. My first question was about the orbit of mediocrity.

"Master, last night, you said if one doesn't practice being in the orbit of mastery, they will end up in the orbit of mediocrity. I want to know more about the orbit of mediocrity."

Master, in his own graceful way, said, "Joy, mastery, and mediocrity are both choices. When you lose sight of what you really want, when you do not consciously practice being in the orbit of mastery, you, by default, end up in the orbit of mediocrity."

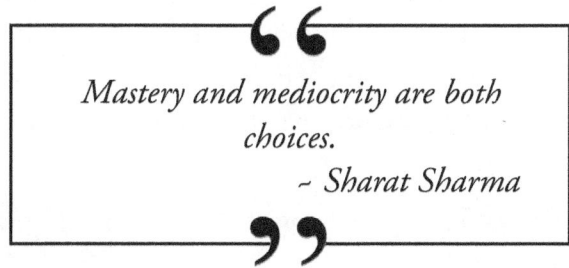

> *Mastery and mediocrity are both choices.*
> *~ Sharat Sharma*

I had no clue about what Master was trying to convey.

Master then asked me, "Joy, you mentioned earlier that there were times when you were successful but felt unhappy, right? Why did you feel so? Have you ever thought of giving up your aspirations, Joy?"

"Honestly, I have been guilty of saying 'I want to give up' several times. There were times when the voices in my head screamed and said things like, 'Nothing will ever work for me. No efforts that I make will ever lead me to the results that I want. There is no point in fighting this hard. I have done all that I can. No one will ever support me. No one really bothers about what I want to do.' And I believed everything that these voices told me. I lost all hope and wanted to give up my aspirations," I confessed.

"The fear of not pursuing my aspirations made me feel shallow and incomplete. Deep within, I felt stuck emotionally and drained psychologically. I was tired of fighting hard, and thoughts of giving up crossed my mind every day. I felt I had done enough and saw no hope in pursuing my aspirations. In fact, I have often imagined the worst."

Master then took a deep sigh and said, "Joy, the truth about humans is that when they feel miserable, they think of every possible thing that can go wrong. It leads them into a negative spiral. They end up believing that all their aspirations of owning a perfect home, being in a great relationship, having a dream job, building a perfect body, or growing a great business will remain a distant hope.

There are many who try to bounce back; they make all possible attempts to resolve every negative feeling they face, but then their imagination makes things worse. It builds an invisible trap for them. The more they try to get back on track, the more they find themselves drifting into this trap. It feels as if you are in quicksand; the more you try to get out, the deeper you sink."

"Yes, I sometimes feel trapped and think that I have no options left," I expressed my despair to Master.

"Well, Joy, this happens because most people never discover their real potential. They never choose to be in the orbit of mastery and hence end up being in the orbit of mediocrity. The first step to mastery is awareness, and the first step to mediocrity is the absence of awareness or ignorance.

When you are ignorant about what is happening in your inner and outer world, you feel disempowered to make the right choices. Your focus gets skewed, and you end up thinking about your limitations than aspirations."

"You mean when I am ignorant about my own strengths, weaknesses, thoughts, beliefs, and values, I am not choosing the right path?"

"Correct!"

"Awareness is the key to be in the orbit of mastery. When I am unaware, I am missing the key to mastery. This lack of awareness is the reason why I end up feeling directionless and meaningless in my pursuit. Is that right, Master?"

"You are right, Joy. This is why most people are successful yet unfulfilled. When you are ignorant, you don't believe in yourself and your aspirations. Everything that others do appeals to you more, and you follow others blindly. You feel that the grass is greener on the other side and miss the fact that the grass is greener wherever you water it."

"I got it, Master. If we are ignorant, we get trapped into believing 'all that glitters is gold', and that is not true."

"That's correct, Joy. While the first step to mediocrity is ignorance, the second step is non-acceptance or denial. When you are ignorant of your strengths, you end up staying in denial of your power. You never access your power and deny taking responsibility for things that you can change. Being in denial creates fear, anxiety, and frustration. All of this leads you further into mediocrity.

Another fact that you must know is that when we deny taking responsibility, we blame, complain, and criticize everything. You feel like a victim, and it further drags you into mediocrity."

Master shared a list of activities that we do when we are unwilling to take responsibility.

1) Catching five extra minutes of sleep when you need to wake up and hit the gym
2) Watching television instead of finishing an important proposal that will get you more business
3) Spending more time in unproductive meetings instead of spending time on execution
4) Munching unhealthy food when you need to eat healthily
5) Buying expensive clothes on discount, using a credit card, when you need to watch your expenses
6) Watching movies on Netflix when you need to spend time socializing and networking with people

"Master, I have done everything that you mentioned. I have denied accessing my power to change and always blamed, complained, and criticized. I have blamed my boss and every other person for my failure; I have complained, stating that other people are luckier than me and also criticized those who are successful."

"It does not really matter what you have done in the past. The moment you become aware, it's your responsibility to accept things and take action. If you stay in denial or don't accept your responsibility, you lead yourself into inaction or inconsistent action. This is the third step in the orbit of mediocrity."

"All of this makes sense now. As you mentioned earlier, this is the negative spiral. Most people are unaware and stay in ignorance of their strengths and the power they hold within. They deny themselves access to these strengths and fail to take complete responsibility. This further leads them to inaction or inconsistent action. They blame, complain, criticize, and never get the results they are searching for. This cycle continues until they learn to break this negative spiral."

"You are correct, Joy, and this decelerates their success further. The thoughts of giving up their aspirations and feeling unfulfilled are because they are in the orbit of mediocrity. Many don't even realize that if they are not progressing, they are regressing. I am reminded of a famous quote I read, 'If you are not growing, you are dying.' That's what happens when you are in the orbit of mediocrity. You decelerate. This is the final step in the orbit of mediocrity.

The moment you find yourself out of the orbit of mastery, you will find yourself in the orbit of mediocrity. All high achievers, elite athletes, global leaders, and successful entrepreneurs understand this, and that's why they consciously choose to be in the orbit of mastery."

Master then said, "This is the foundation for everything you want to build in your life. Whether you want to be a successful entrepreneur or a working professional, you must choose mastery over mediocrity. Mastery is the ultimate choice that will make you successful and fulfilled."

Orbit of Mediocrity

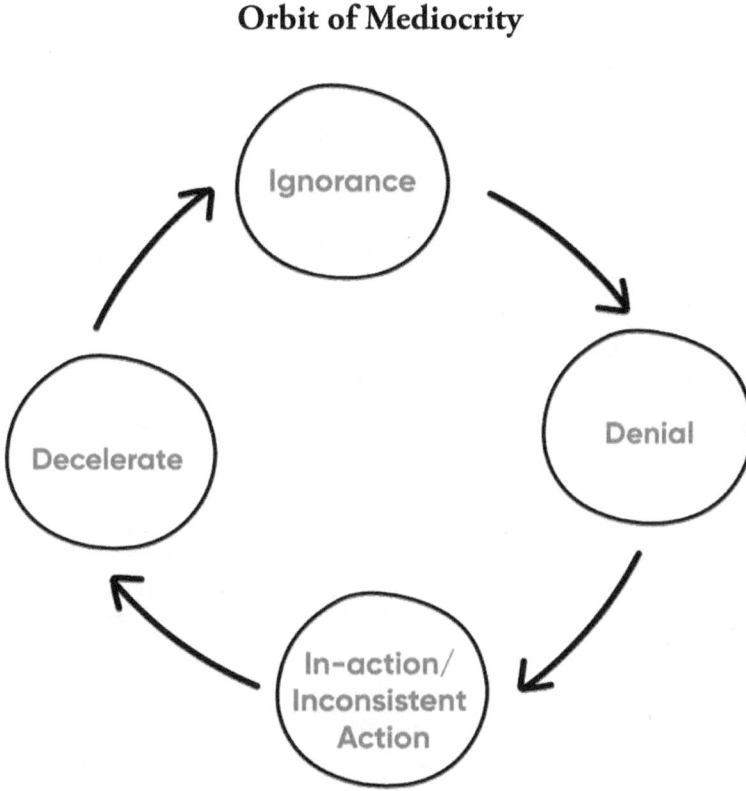

This was the foundation of every lesson that Master shared over the next few days. Being aware of the orbit of mastery and the orbit of mediocrity gave me a blueprint to understand and choose mastery over mediocrity. I made a commitment to practice being in the orbit of mastery for the rest of my life.

We spoke for some time and then decided to continue our conversation in the evening. We planned to meet near the pond. I went back to my room and introspected on all the insights that Master had shared.

In the evening ...

We met in the evening and exchanged a few random thoughts. I shared with Master everything that I felt about this mystic and beautiful place. He recognized the fact that I was happier amidst the mountains. Master then mentioned that many successful people had come to visit this land to find answers to their questions. It is said that this mystic land filled with silence has helped many find answers to their questions.

The 'One' Invisible Code

After some time, with all my curiosity, I asked, "Master, what else makes all the high achievers different from us? Why are they considered exceptional? Is there something they know that many don't?"

Master looked at me and said, "They are not exceptions; they are great examples of what human potential is capable of!"

Master continued, "Be it Ali Baba or Ratan Tata as entrepreneurs, Roger Federer or M. S. Dhoni as sportsmen, Will Smith or Amitabh Bachchan as global icons, or many others, they are examples to understand what the human potential is capable of. All of them define what is possible for humans. Many consider them exceptions, but the truth is, they are one among us. When you think of them as exceptions, you think they are different and feel insecure. When you think of them as examples, you are ready to learn from them."

I always thought of these highly successful people as people who were naturally gifted, more talented, or had inherited loads of good fortune. But I never thought of them as examples of human potential.

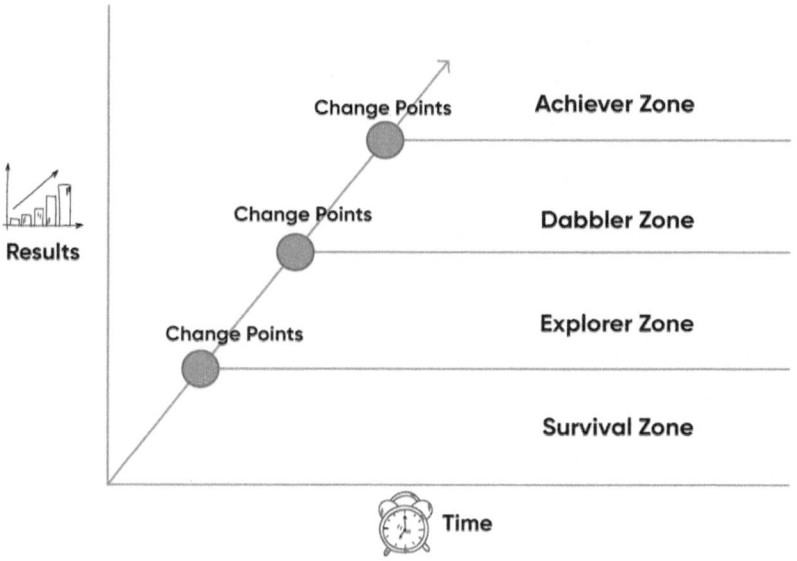

Master said, "What I am going to tell you in the next few days will help you understand how these people tapped into their potential and achieved results, and how they have set an example for many to follow."

Master then started scribbling something on a sheet of paper and said, "Time and results—these are the two variables on which we draw the trajectory of our success. We all start with big aspirations, but with time, we either live or limit our potential."

"What do you mean by live or limit our potential?"

"Joy, when you pursue your aspirations and want to succeed, you have to change at regular intervals. A lot of people think that the recipe for success and growth is to be in the right place at the right time with the right skills. But then they forget about being the right person with the right mindset. When you have the right mindset, you are open to change and that lets you live your potential, but when you don't have the right mindset, you are reluctant to change and you end up limiting your potential.

Remember this, Joy, every different level of success will need a different mindset. If you don't change and adapt, you will get stuck, and that's how the trajectory of your success gets defined.

PART 2

CHAPTER 4

FINDING YOUR ROAR – THE MINDSET

Muhammad Ali once said, 'It isn't the mountains ahead to climb that wear you out. It's the pebble in your shoe.' Imagine walking a mile on tough terrain. You are willing to risk everything when you are passionate and driven by the destination you want to reach. But the mile ahead feels impossible when there is a pebble in your shoe. That's exactly how our life shapes up. In our journey, pebbles show up in the form of our mindset. These create resistance and show up as what-ifs, could-have-beens, and never-going-to-bes.

>
> *'It isn't the mountains ahead to climb that wear you out. It's the pebble in your shoe.'*
> ~ Muhammad Ali
>

Like the pebbles that stop you from climbing, it is the mindset that stops you from changing. In order to reach your potential, you must know what kind of mindset dominates in you and how this mindset is fueling or burning your aspirations."

"Master, how do I know my current mindset?"

Master explained, "Joy, there are two forces that shape your life — aspiration of the future and our current mindset. Our mindset is the beliefs and values that we have about ourselves and others. Most people are unaware that it is our mindset that can make us or break us. When we are focused only on setting our aspirations and are not building our mindset, we experience temporary success. I say this because, as soon as we face a setback, a poor mindset gives up aspirations."

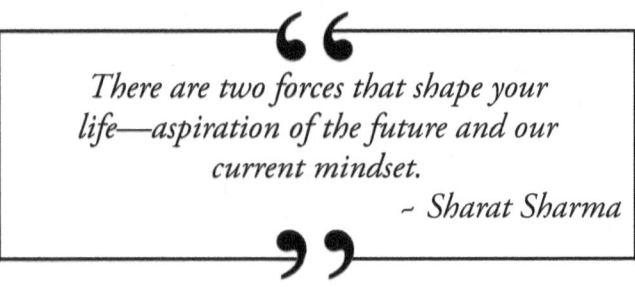

> *There are two forces that shape your life—aspiration of the future and our current mindset.*
> ~ Sharat Sharma

"Do you mean those who have the right mindset don't face setbacks?"

"We all face setbacks, but then the ones with a powerful mindset choose to make a comeback while others don't. Tim Gallwey, in his book *The Inner Game of Work*, talks about the performance formula. He says each of us possess the potential to accomplish great things in life. However, our performances match our potential only when we eliminate resistance."

Performance = Potential − Resistance

Master continued to explain. "Higher the resistance, lower is the performance. Then it does not really matter how much potential you possess; your performance will be impacted by all the resistance that you face. While it is easy to disguise oneself and say that the resistance is external, in reality, the resistance comes from within. Internal resistance is the negative voices that are part of your mindset. These voices hold you back from doing things that matter. These voices gain momentum when you start aiming big. If you listen to these voices, you hold yourselves back from taking action."

"What other impact does my mindset have on me?" I asked.

Master smiled and said, "Your current mindset is a result of all the conditioning you go through in your life. It is how you think and what you believe. It creates a set of perceptions and assumptions about you and others. It constantly influences your everyday decisions and actions. It defines how you respond to events and circumstances. It shapes your present and contributes to building your future."

"Can you give me an example of this, Master?" I asked.

Then Master narrated a beautiful story to explain how we create our lives.

A little tiger cub lost his parents at birth. The poor cub wandered around for a few days and then came upon a flock of sheep. Now, this little baby tiger was not threatening to these sheep. So, they took in the tiger and raised him as their own. Soon the tiger cub grew large, as tigers generally do. But, instead of feasting on the food that other tigers ate, this tiger ate grass just like the sheep.

One day, a big male adult tiger was hunting for food when he came across the sheep. His eyes sticking just above the grass, the big male tiger scanned the flock, looking for the tastiest meal. What did the hungry tiger see? He saw a big, adolescent tiger eating grass. Whenever the adolescent tiger paused, he lifted up his head and said, "Baaaa."

"Oh no," thought the adult tiger. At once, he pounced upon the herd, as though he had been released from cannon. The big cat easily nabbed two sheep in an instant. The junior tiger looked up at the adult and swallowed his grass.

The big male sauntered over to the junior tiger and said, "Kid, what happened?" All that the young tiger could say was, "Baaaa." The adult tiger thought to himself, "This is totally unacceptable." Then he took that young tiger back to his cave. The first thing he did was cut open one of the sheep he had nabbed. Then the adult tiger shoved a paw full of meat into the young tiger's mouth. Having never tasted meat his whole life, do you know what he did? He threw up all over the cave floor.

Well, in time, our young friend grew accustomed to the taste of the tiger's diet. He ate meat heartily and happily. He learned to hunt silently, to be still, and to attack with ferocity. The most impressive thing our big tiger friend learned was to open his jaws and roar—a roar that could reverberate throughout the fullness of the jungle and shake every animal to its core. In time, the young tiger grew into a very large adult, who roamed and ruled its territory as every tiger desires.

"This story is a great reminder that we need to know how our mindset is shaped, how what we believe about ourselves limits us from being who we are meant to be, and how many of us live like sheep, having forgotten to roar."

Master and I had a great laugh as we discussed how many of us have forgotten how to roar and continue to bleat like a sheep.

I thought about how I have been a sheep many times, and not a tiger. Half my life, I had believed the things that others told me to believe. I guess many of us do this. But now was the time for me to roar, I decided. I had to stop baaing and start roaring. I had to change.

Knowing Your Mindset

Finding the roar or knowing who you are is the key to your success. Knowing who you are is to be aware of your current mindset. This must be the top priority of every individual, entrepreneur, and corporate leader. When you know your current mindset, you can consciously choose to change and sail through any adversity that life throws at you.

I have observed that, in the face of challenges, we question our abilities and invest our time only in improving them. We ignore the need to develop our mindset. We don't understand that abilities can be learned and improved, but the differentiator is always the mindset. Developing only the abilities is like working on the symptoms and not on the root cause. The root cause of every success is the mindset.

Master then introduced me to the four types of mindsets and how they shape our results and our aspirations.

Four types of mindsets

Survivor mindset

"Joy, most people die at the age of 17 but get buried only at 70. It means that they are merely surviving between 17 and 70."

I replied instantly, "I agree, Master. I have seen many people who never pursue their aspirations and never discover their potential. Pursuing these aspirations can make them happy and fulfilled, but then they never pursue them because they are stuck reacting to life challenges."

"The truth is, most people don't set strong aspirations and don't trust their potential. As a result, when they face challenges, they get too caught in reacting to these challenges and lose sight of their aspirations. When you do not have a strong aspiration, you let fear influence you easily. Every decision you make then is to avoid mistakes and not to align yourself with the aspirations. You are busy fixing things than building them. You end up not taking the risk and miss out on the fact that there is no reward without risk."

"I agree, Master!"

"That's how a survival mindset works. With a survivor mindset, societal norms take precedence over everything else, and you end up believing that risking more, aiming higher, and trying harder will only disappoint you. This is what society teaches you. Even when you wish to aim higher, you are in constant fear of being judged and rejected. You then start conforming to society. For the rest of your life, you live based on the beliefs and values of society."

"So, do you mean when someone has a survivor mindset, they do not set big aspirations?"

"Well, with the survivor mindset, you do start with big aspirations, but when you face challenges, you get busier in controlling the challenges.

These challenges demand you to change, but then you are reluctant to change. Every change requires you to shift your mindset and learn new skills. With a survivor mindset, you don't give significance to learning and growing. When you don't learn and never change, you sabotage your own aspirations."

"Joy, what drives our action is our emotions. The emotion that drives a survivor mindset is fear, and that's exactly why they avoid challenges, find opportunities as threats, constantly worry about judgments and criticism of others, compare themselves with others, and feel threatened. In the presence of competition, they belittle themselves.

A survivor mindset rationalizes the reasons for not reaching their aspirations and living their potential by

- ❖ Playing the victim card: I am not at fault.
- ❖ Blaming others: It's the people around me.
- ❖ Avoiding: I don't need this, I am comfortable!
- ❖ Negating: I just need to go with the flow.
- ❖ Invalidating by comparing: Most people don't do this; so, it's not really necessary.
- ❖ Staying in denial: It's not necessary, and if it is, I will figure it out myself."

I asked, "What else stops them from changing their mindset?"

Master said, "Joy, most of our behavior is motivated by our need to avoid pain and repeat the activities that give us pleasure. A person with a survivor mindset associates pleasure with the things that give a sense of comfort in the present and considers change painful."

"How long will someone hold on to this mindset of a being a survivor?"

"As long as they choose to, Joy. You may have understood by now that when someone is just surviving, it is because they have given up their power to other people and circumstances. This simply means that as long as they let their life get defined by others and life circumstances, they may remain survivors. If they do not consciously expand their awareness and learn to change faster, if they do not accept full responsibility for their lives, they will continue to survive."

"So, what should someone with a survivor mindset do?"

Master continued after a brief pause, "If you identify yourself with this mindset, then you must know that there is no accidental growth. That is why you must focus on driving growth intentionally. Set aspirations that are powerful. You must learn to change faster and expand your self-awareness. Identify and challenge the non-supportive beliefs and values that are keeping you stuck." (More on challenging and changing beliefs in the next chapter)

Actions to change Survival Mindset:
- ❖ Drive growth intentionally
- ❖ Set powerful aspirations
- ❖ Identify and challenge the beliefs that are holding you back

Explorer mindset

Master then said, "There are many who strive hard and break through the survivor mindset."

Master asked, "Do you start projects but never complete them? Do you feel motivated at the beginning of the project, but then the motivation does not stay for too long? Do you constantly keep searching for the next project that can give you that adrenaline rush? Do you get caught between multiple projects and feel overwhelmed and lost?"

I smiled and said, "That sounds a lot like me, Master."

"Joy, welcome to the world of an explorer mindset. Explorers change when the challenges show up, but then their focus gets skewed, and they end up doing things that keep them busy not fulfilled. They are unsure where all the busyness is leading them. When you have an explorer mindset and you face challenges, you get busy trying every solution that comes your way. You get easily distracted by popular things, and real, meaningful aspirations do not capture your attention.

As an explorer, you may see success in the short-term, but as soon as you find something more appealing, you get carried away. You get caught in the shiny object syndrome and think all that glitters is gold. You end up sacrificing your personal aspirations for the popular things of society. As a result, you hop from one project to another without completing any of them."

I remarked, "I can relate to this, Master. I am always caught between my internal struggles and societal demands. I do set a big aspiration for myself, but then I get carried away by the next big thing that everyone is talking about. I consider the big thing to be more important than the aspiration I have set for myself. A lot of times, I notice that other people's aspirations become my aspiration. I get caught between what I want and what everyone is chasing. I also remember how my friend diversified his business once and started other services that were easy to sell. He did that only because everyone was doing it. But then he lost focus from the main product and lost money when he diversified. I also notice my friends going from one popular thing to another and never sticking to one."

"Joy, not setting powerful aspirations or getting carried away by other people's aspirations is as good as having no aspiration. Chasing multiple aspirations is akin to chasing two rabbits and catching none.

People with explorer mindset disguise themselves by being busy in many unimportant things. They are afraid of facing the current situation, which demands them to change. While they want to change, they are afraid of judgment and non-acceptance from others. Constant 'what-ifs' rule their life—what if I fail, what if things go wrong, what if others don't like it, what if I get rejected—these are the constant thoughts that control their actions. And that's why they choose to take the safe path of following what everyone else is doing.

A lot of times, you will find explorers basking in the glory of their past achievements, however minor or accidental. I say accidental achievements because they happen accidentally and not intentionally. When your focus gets distorted from the major aspirations that you are chasing to the minor achievements, you distract yourself into mediocre results."

"I see myself as someone with an explorer mindset. But what is holding me back from setting a powerful aspiration and sticking to it?"

"Joy, you get affected by distractions because you believe that the grass is greener on the other side. You are not focused on what your aspirations can make you; you are busy watching over the fence to see what others aspire for and think that can inspire you too. When you do not have clear, powerful aspirations, you get easily overpowered by other people's aspirations."

"So, what should I do?"

"Accept full responsibility for discovering your full potential. Expand your self-awareness and set powerful aspirations. As you do that, you will be driven by the aspirations that you have set and not get distracted by things that appeal to you in the short run. Pursue your aspirations intentionally and make conscious choices that align with your aspirations.

When you invest your energy in discovering your full potential, you stop getting influenced by other people's aspirations. You develop a single-minded focus and feel inspired by your aspiration. You now direct all your energy in fulfilling your aspirations. Remember Joy, the grass is greener on the other side is a half-truth; the complete truth is the grass is greener where you water it."

> *The difference between what we do and what we are capable of doing would solve most of the world's problems.*
> *~ Mahatma Gandhi*

This was a profound lesson for me. I had been an explorer all my life, and I had always thought that the grass was greener on the other side. I did not realize that the grass is greener where I water it. All this while, I did not spend time on my aspirations and allowed my focus to get distorted by other people's success. I jumped onto things that were popular than the things that were meaningful. It was time that I set my mindset and my aspirations right.

> "If you identify yourself with this mindset, these are some actions that you must take."
> - ❖ Relentlessly explore your potential
> - ❖ Stay focused on your aspirations
> - ❖ Develop a single-minded focus
> - ❖ Remember, the grass is greener where you water it

Dabbler mindset

> *The tragedy of life is often not in our failure, but rather in our complacency; not in our doing too much, but rather in our doing too little; not in our living above our ability, but rather in our living below our capacities.*
> *~ Benjamin E. Mays*

Master began, "Let's talk about the next mindset, which is the dabbler mindset. Those with a dabbler mindset are aware of their potential, and they set big aspirations. They constantly anticipate building a great future. However, they hold themselves back while executing with consistency. The dabbler mindset gets complacent after achieving certain results.

They talk about big goals, but when it comes to taking consistent action, they let comfort hijack them. Their action gives them short-term result, which makes them feel content for a short while. Soon the short-lived contentment turns into unfulfillment. The mismatch between big aspirations and actions does not allow them to experience every result that's possible. When you constantly think that you are capable of more but do not execute, you end up with the feeling of unfulfillment."

"Isn't that self-sabotaging?" I questioned.

"Yes, this is self-sabotaging behavior. The more you do this, you end up lowering your self-worth. This eventually becomes a pattern to safeguard yourself. When you feel content with what you have achieved, you let complacency kick in."

"What is complacency?"

"Complacency is the habit you learn every time you give up too soon. When you become too complacent, you do not pursue your aspirations with the same vigor with which you set them."

"What drives a dabbler?"

"It is usually the thought, 'if I can achieve the next target, I will be fine'. And when you achieve that target, instead of setting a bigger target, you become complacent with what you have achieved. Until one day, when reality hits you and demands you to set a bigger target. In fact, a lot of dabblers unknowingly develop certain undesirable characteristics."

Master delved deep into these undesirable traits.

Sense of entitlement: Having seen success in the past, dabblers believe that this success will guarantee them success in the future too. They believe that they deserve admiration and respect because of the success they have already achieved. At times, this manifests itself as anger. They demand rewards without hard work.

Narrow focus: The key to success is to focus on the future and continue to take action in the present. But dabblers dilute this by focusing only on the present and taking action to fulfill the present. They succumb to instant gratification and get lost in doing things that give them temporary pleasure. They do not attempt tasks that give them long-term fulfillment. There is a constant battle between what they want now and what they want the most. The battle is won by the former.

Stop learning and listening: Dabblers get complacent and take their success for granted. They fail to learn, unlearn, and relearn. They think that they know everything and have tried everything. They are busy celebrating their past success and do not tune to the swift changes happening in the world.

Master then got back to what he was explaining earlier. "Those with the dabbler mindset let complacency affect them so much that their own passion soon turns into poison. They get careless with a false sense of pride due to past success."

"What should the dabbler do?" I asked.

"The dabbler must find the courage to accept that growth happens when we focus all our energy on our future aspirations. They must not get too complacent about their present achievements. Dabblers must transcend from being dabblers to achievers; this can happen only when they take responsibility for every action. Every time they reach a target, they must set a bigger one and strive to achieve it."

I was able to connect with every word Master had said. I started to think about how most people keep switching between the mindsets of survivor, explorer, and dabbler.

Master said, "Only when you trust your potential and are driven by your aspiration, you give yourself permission to reach your potential."

> "Only when you trust your potential and are driven by your aspiration, you give yourself permission to reach your potential."
> ~ Sharat Sharma

These mindsets were a big revelation to me.

> If you identify yourself with this mindset, these are some actions that you must take.
> - ❖ Set a powerful execution process
> - ❖ Review your actions and measure your outcomes
> - ❖ Identify and challenge the beliefs that are holding you back

Achiever mindset

"Achievers are those who are deeply aligned with their aspirations and continue to take action. As an achiever, you match your every aspiration with relentless execution. You walk the talk and exemplify authenticity. You not only motivate others with words but also inspire them with your actions. Staying focused on the future and taking action in the present is the quality that drives you. You never settle for what you get and are always raising the bar. This is what defines an achiever mindset," elaborated Master.

"What else do achievers do?" I asked.

"People with an achiever mindset are always playing for the next level of success. They have a strong desire to create a positive impact with their potential. The achiever mindset understands that if they see too far into the future, they will feel anxious. They also know that if they cling to their past, they will feel fearful. So, they practice being in the present and continue to take action. Let me explain this.

The white rhinoceros can weigh up to 3,500 kg, and its front horn can grow up to 150 cm in length. But their bulk doesn't hold them back though, as rhinos can run at a speed of 56 kmph, as fast as a galloping horse. To put this in context, the world's fastest man, Usain Bolt, runs at approximately 38 kmph. Such size and speed may be scary, but their eyesight is so poor that an immobile person is undetectable to a rhino from a distance of 30 meters. Imagine half a dozen three-ton rhinos with massive horns, running at over 50 kmph! But they cannot see more than 30 meters in front of them. Amazing, right? You must get out of their way, or you will be crushed! That's what happens when latent potential turns into incredible power without worrying too far ahead. Achievers are like rhinos; they crush everything that comes in their way by being present at opportunities."

"What drives achievers?"

"Achievers are hungry and are always aiming for the next level of success. As they reach one milestone, they readily set another one. They are highly committed to making plans proactively and executing them. One of the key traits of an achiever is crafting one's own path and not getting influenced by others around. They proactively change with time. Achievers are aware of the fact that we all get influenced by the company we keep. Hence, they choose to be with other achievers and get influenced by their positivity. They are also constantly learning and expanding their levels of awareness. They understand that growth has to be intentional and cannot be accidental."

"Got it now, Master. Only when we strive to develop an achievers mindset, we will be able to live our full potential," I shared.

I was unaware of my mindset, and now I knew that my mindset didn't align with my aspirations. I now understood that having potential is one thing, but believing in the potential and constantly working on strengthening the mindset is the key to breaking through mediocrity and reaching the next level of personal and professional success.

It was evening, and we decided to head back.

I then asked, "Master, why do only a few people develop achievers mindset?"

"Joy, one of the keys that contribute to building an achievers mindset is the ability to own the truth about life and success. These truths are like certain principles. While most people shy away from accepting these truths, achievers own them"

We decided to meet the next day in Master's study room.

The Four Mindsets

Survival Mindset
Living for self
Fear controls them
Refuse to learn & change

Explorer Mindset
Living for others
Get influenced by others
Always think grass is greener on the other side

Achiever Mindset
Living for bigger purpose
What more can I achieve?
Learning and changing is the essence of life

Dabbler Mindset
Living for short-term results
Chasing the next big thing will give me happiness
Fail to learn and change faster

The Battle That We Fight Within

CHAPTER 5

OWNING THE TRUTH

I got up early and reached Master's study room. I noticed that Master had an amazing collection of books in his library. I waited for Master.

As Master arrived, we started talking about high achievers. He said, "Joy, all high achievers own certain truths. These truths are the principles that help them create exemplary results. They never go back on any of these truths. Many of these truths are unconventional and will need you to think beyond what you have learned so far. This means you must unlearn. Are you ready to unlearn and own these truths?"

We spent the whole day discussing the truths and how to **Own the Truth.**

Truth #1: Problems come to refine us, not define us

Master said, "Problems and challenges are an integral part of every growth story. When you face problems, you can choose to escape from the problems or learn from these problems. All high achievers know that it is problems that enable them to grow and reach their full potential. They know that bigger aspirations are bound to bring bigger problems, and they grow in proportion to the problems they solve.

Many of us believe that we should never face problems. But, in reality, it is problems that shape us into better individuals. They happen only to refine us and not define us. Every high achiever knows and owns this truth."

"I want to understand this more," I said inquisitively.

"Joy, problems don't happen to you; they happen for you. When you think that problems happen to you, you let yourself get defined by them. When you understand that problems happen for you, you exercise your power to face them. You learn to respond and not react to the problems. As you respond, you learn several lessons. The more lessons you learn, the more aware you become of your potential. You understand that what matters the most is not the thing that happens to you but how you respond to it. The more problems you solve, the more you recognize that you are bigger than the problems you face, and you have the potential to solve every problem.

In simple words, when you solve the problem, you get refined as a person, your awareness expands, your thoughts are clear, your confidence boosts, and a lot of great things happen. But when you don't solve the problem, you assume that you are incapable, and that's how you let these problems define you."

Everything that Master was sharing was beginning to make absolute sense.

"When you face problems, you can find reasons to escape and complain, or look for the lessons and grow. Every time you face a problem, you have a choice of saying – why me or try me."

"What happens when we refuse to learn the lesson?"

Master smiled and said, "The storm that doesn't make you strong will always return. When we refuse to learn or stay in denial, the problem repeats itself until we learn. That's the best part about these problems.

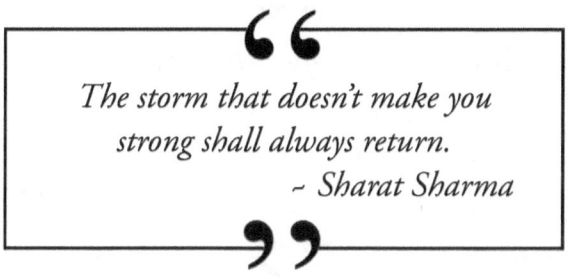

The storm that doesn't make you strong shall always return.
~ Sharat Sharma

High achievers also know how to recognize the problems faster. They are aware that problems often appear as resistance, hesitation, or as a feeling of being stuck. Every time they are in any such situation, they take a pause and ask: What am I supposed to learn from this problem?"

Master, in his own charismatic way, said, "Joy, have you ever seen a fly stuck in a bottle? Did you notice how it tries to make all attempts to fly out of the bottle? It does anything and everything to escape but then only finds itself hitting the walls of the bottle. It tries harder to find a narrow opening but fails. It keeps trying hard until it eventually gives up and dies in the bottle. Most people are like the fly. They try to battle with problems every day, and in the end, they find themselves tired and unfulfilled."

"I agree and relate to this, Master."

"In this battle, there are those who want to conquer everything that's outside of them, and then there are those who are fighting and winning the battle within. This constant battle is where the trajectory of life gets defined. This is where one decides to reach their full potential and become a high performer or settle as a mediocre. The truth is, those who win the battle within can never be defeated. They are the ones who redefine the word 'success' and always inspire others. They are high achievers. Those who are fighting the battle outside are often fighting an endless battle. They perspire and never reach their full potential. The internal battle is won by constantly asking one simple question - *What can I learn?*"

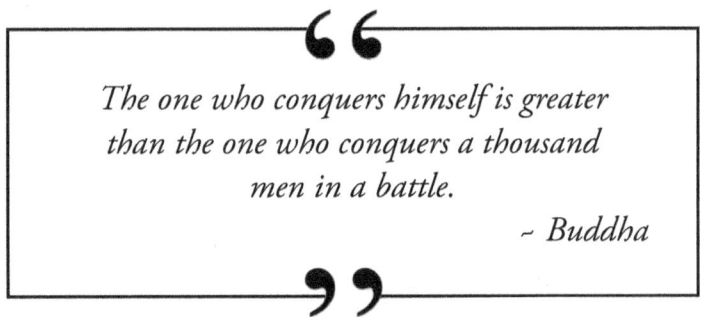

> *The one who conquers himself is greater than the one who conquers a thousand men in a battle.*
> ~ Buddha

I then said, "Master, I now understand the meaning of what you said: *Problems come to refine us and not define us*, and why every high achiever owns this truth. They know that they will face problems, and they are aware that all they need to ask is: What can I learn? The sooner they learn, the sooner they tap into their potential."

Master then asked, "Do you know people who don't have any problems?"

I shrugged my shoulders, expressing my disbelief in such a possibility.

Master said, "The only people without problems are in cemeteries."

As Master said that, we both burst into laughter.

> *The only people without problems are in cemeteries.*
> *~ Tony Robbins*

Inspiration Corner

Rowling, the author of the successful fantasy series, Harry Potter, *did not have an easy life. She was a self-proclaimed failure, a single, divorced parent, who was bankrupt and living on welfare when she wrote the first three chapters of the Harry Potter book. She had hit rock bottom and was clinically depressed. She put all this in her only solace—writing.*

Even after submitting the manuscript to a dozen publishers, Rowling did not have any luck, until finally an editor at Bloomsbury Publishing House in London decided to publish the book after his eight-year-old daughter read the first chapter and immediately demanded to read the rest of the book.

Then Rowling was informed that she would need a day job as there would not be any money in children's books.

The rest is history as the Harry Potter series won several awards, was translated in over 80 languages and sold over 400 million copies! The books in the series have been made into movies as well.

The Harry Potter books are not only bestselling books, but they also gained recognition for sparking an interest in reading among the young, at a time when children were thought to be abandoning books for computers and television. Today, Rowling is one of the richest and most influential authors in Britain. And she credits much of her success to her failure.

Rowling said in a Harvard commencement speech, "Failure meant stripping away of the inessential. I stopped pretending to myself that I was anything other than what I was and began to direct all my energy to finish the only work that mattered to me. Had I really succeeded at anything else, I might never have found the determination to succeed in the one area where I truly belonged. I was set free because my greatest fear had been realized, and I was still alive, and I still had a daughter whom I adored, and I had an old typewriter and a big idea. And so rock bottom became a solid foundation on which I rebuilt my life."

It is impossible to live without failing at something unless you live so cautiously that you might as well not have lived at all – in which case, you fail by default.

~ J. K. Rowling

Truth #2: Your Choices Shape Your Life

After an insightful discussion on the first truth, Master and I decided to take a walk. The cold breeze and intense conversation was a perfect match. Master had a great way of simplifying things, and that's the thing I liked about our conversations.

I asked Master why people believed in limitations and did not make intelligent choices.

To this, Master said, "Joy, the truth is, every result that you see in your life is shaped by the choices you make. Some exercise their choices and feel free, but many never exercise their choices and feel chained to their limitations. Every high achiever knows and owns the truth that our life is shaped by the choices we make. Let me share an inspiring incident that changed my life."

***

It was a couple of years ago. I had visited Hyderabad on a late-night flight. After reaching the airport, I found the taxi stand to be unusually deserted. Later, I got to know that most of the taxi drivers were participating in an ongoing strike. I waited for almost 30 minutes with the hope of finding a taxi. With no sight of any taxi, my hope started fading. So, I decided to call my friends for help. Then I heard a husky voice from behind, "Sir, where do you want to go?"

A well-built man in his 40s walked up to me, smiled, and said, "Sir, there is a taxi strike, and you will not find any taxi here." I was a little perplexed by his approach and found something very intriguing about him. Even before I could think and say something, he said, "My taxi is parked at some distance," and extended his card. It read, 'Mr. RK (MA – English)' with additional details. We spoke for a while, and he offered to drop me at my destination.

These few minutes of interaction, his unusual style, and his world-class English stumped me and raised a lot of questions in my mind. (Taxi drivers speaking in English are not usual in this part of the world.)

I had heard of taxi drivers who took advantage of the airport's distance from the city to fleece travelers, especially if they were traveling late at night. I had also heard of the modus operandi used by taxi drivers—they are very polite and use extraordinary communication skills to impress and then loot their customers.

I had a choice to make—either trust him and reach home or wait for someone to pick me up. I was doubtful, yet I chose the first option.

The voice in my mind said, "Was I going to regret this decision?"

Little did I ever imagine that the next 45 minutes would turn out to be one of the most interesting and inspiring 45 minutes of my life.

As we started heading towards the destination, Mr. RK tried to initiate a conversation and made some general inquiries.

I asked him, "Do you hold a Master's degree in English?"

Mr. RK said, "Yes, I completed it when I was in jail."

There was silence. I asked myself again, "Am I going to regret making this choice?"

M. RK said, "I was convicted of murder and was in jail for five years."

There was a long bout of silence this time.

Mr. RK sensed my apprehension and said, "It happened when there were riots. It was the same riots where I lost my family. I was jailed for five years. I was 20 and passionate about my studies."

"And then, what happened?"

Mr. RK smiled and said, "I just remained positive and finished my studies while I was in jail."

"But why did you kill people?"

Mr. RK replied with a smile, "I did not."

"What!?"

And then there was silence again.

I asked, "Weren't you scared?"

Mr. RK smiled at me and said, "Yes, it was scary. I was abused and assaulted every day. I wanted to give up my life. I even decided to commit suicide. Then something strange happened. One day, I heard a voice. I heard the voice of my mother. My mother had always been my inspiration. She had always told me that each morning when I woke up, I had a choice. I could choose to go back to sleep or wake up and start chasing my dream. I chose to chase my dream. When something bad happens, I can choose to be a victim, or I can choose to learn from the experience and be a hero. I chose to learn and be a hero. I can choose to be in comfort or choose to stretch and accept challenges. I chose to stretch and accept challenges. When facing struggles, I can choose to complain or look for the positive side of life. I chose to see the positive side of life."

"Yeah, right, but it's not that easy when you have tough circumstances or difficult people around you. Look at you. You were jailed for NO reason!" I protested.

Mr. RK again smiled and said, "I never believed when my mother told me that everything is a choice. But then the truth is, when you cut away all the junk, every situation is a choice. You choose how you react to situations. You choose how people will affect your mood. You choose to be a victim or a hero. The bottom line is that we always have a choice. When I was in jail, I only remembered the voice of my mother. Today I live with my wonderful family, own a fleet of cars, and the only reason I am not in jail is because I made a choice."

There was silence until I reached my destination.

***

"Every time I sit back and think about RK, I wonder how he never accepted the limitations that were imposed upon him. He knew that he always had a choice. From being in jail to owning a fleet of cars, that's quite something! He never got stuck. He always learned to exercise his choices."

I said, "That's truly inspiring, Master!"

"This is what high achievers do. They always exercise their choices. The truth is, we earn a certain level of income, live a certain standard of life, build a great business, and have great relationships because of our choices. We all must own this truth. We must understand that it is our choices that shape our lives."

I felt that I made the right choice to be with Master and learn from him. This choice had already taught me so many lessons. I was committed to owning this truth.

We decided to walk back, and as we reached the house, I noticed that many guests were waiting to meet Master.

We decided to end the day and meet the next day.

Inspiration Corner

Srikanth Bolla was born blind in a small village called Sitaramapuram in Andhra Pradesh, where illiteracy was rampant and being born blind was considered a sin. Born to parents who refused to give him up, Srikanth not only managed to finish his education from Massachusetts Institute of Technology (MIT) but also created a Rs. 70 crores company.

At the age of seven, Srikanth moved away from home, learned Braille, English, and how to use a computer. He topped his 10th board exams and decided to study Science instead of Arts, as was expected from a blind student. Adamant about studying only Science, Srikanth filed a case against the Andhra Pradesh Board of Secondary Education, which refused to admit a blind student to the Science stream. He won the case and finished his 12th boards securing 98%.

However, he wasn't done yet. Refusing to bow down, he applied to universities in the United States (U.S.), after he was denied an admit card to write the Indian Institute of Technology's entrance exam. Not only was his application accepted in the U.S., he was also accepted in four of the most prestigious colleges in the world today—MIT, Stanford, Berkeley, and Carnegie Mellon. He was the first international blind student to be given a place at MIT.

At the Massachusetts Institute of Technology, he started a center with the staff for the visually challenged to learn computer skills through a 10-week computer course. After completing his education from MIT, the prodigal son returned to India with an intention to make a difference in the lives of people who suffer from disabilities.

He first started a nonprofit organization, Samanvai, for students with multiple disabilities. Samanvai aims to provide individualized, need-based, goal-oriented support services for students with disabilities to get proper education. Around 3,000 students have been helped, nurtured, and mentored by Srikanth through Samanvai.

In 2012, he decided to take the next big step for the betterment of not just unskilled laborers and disabled people, but also for the environment. This step was the establishment of Bollant Industries Pvt. Ltd., which had a threefold purpose. First, to help unskilled and uneducated disabled people, second, to encash agricultural waste from farmers, and finally, stop environmental degradation because of the excess use of plastic and Styrofoam.

Today, Bollant Industries has five manufacturing plants that produce eco-friendly products such as areca leaf plates, cups, trays, and dinnerware. They also manufacture betel plates and disposable plates, spoons, cups, adhesives, and printing products. Manufacturing giant, Ratan Tata, also invested an undisclosed amount in the company, and Srini Raju of Peepul Capital and Satish Reddy of Dr. Reddy's Laboratories are a part of the company's board. India's top angel investor, Ravi Mantha, not only invested in Srikanth's mission but also became his mentor and is presently the director and financial advisor of Bollant Industries.

Bollant Industries' sales cross 70 million per year and employ over 150 disabled individuals catering to local and international customers. An inspiration to many people around the world, Srikanth Bolla believes that if you do something good, it will come back to you.

Srikanth Bolla's story is a true story of inspiration, not just because of the hurdles he faced and conquered, but because of his continuing battle with the world to provide better opportunities to people with multiple disabilities.

Truth #3: Your Self-Worth Defines Your Net worth

It was a fresh new morning. I got up early and went for a jog. I was glad to see Master on the jogging track. I wished him good morning and joined him. The inquisitive me could not hold back and started engaging in a conversation with Master.

"Master, I want to ask you a question," I said.

"Go ahead, Joy," said Master.

"Master, often, we hear that we must believe in our own capabilities. I remember you told me that most achievers are just examples and not exceptions. But then we cannot deny the fact that there are many others who are better than us. They are competent, handle fear well, make the right choice always, and are prepared to handle any adversities. Aren't they better than me? I always have this question, and I often feel intimidated in their presence."

Master smiled and said, "Imagine this, Joy. You and your friend want to build a beautiful garden. So, one day, both of you decide to buy some seeds and plant them in the garden. Your friend plants his seed in his garden and you in yours. You work hard, water the seeds, and take care of the seeds with all the necessary fertilizers and minerals every day. You do this tirelessly and wait, but then the seeds do not turn into plants. You feel a little disappointed. Then one day, you decide to visit your friend. You notice that the seeds in his garden have turned into beautiful plants. Your friend is happy. You think he worked harder than you, and that's why his seeds turned into plants.

Though you feel disappointed, you choose not to give up. You start taking care of the seeds in your garden with a lot more patience. You spend more time with the seeds. But as time passes, you still see no results. Now you are dejected. You notice that your friend's plants have started to turn into big, beautiful trees. Everyone admires the trees and praises your neighbor. You feel rejected and give up on watering your seeds. You stop believing that your seeds will turn into plants. You start cursing your friend and call him lucky.

Just when you are planning to give up, you notice that the seeds that you had sown have turned into small plants. You feel delighted, and then within a few days, they turn into big plants. Now you do not complain, and you do not think that your friend was lucky. Instead, you focus on your victory.

But then, you may ask what happened to the seed all these days? Why did the seeds not turn into a tree? The answer is simple. The seeds were busy spreading and strengthening their roots. That's what the seed is meant to be. All this while the seeds did not compare itself with another seed, the tree did not compare itself with another tree and feel disappointed; it did not complain. This is the exact thing that we must do, Joy. We must stop comparing, complaining, and feeling disappointed. We must focus on doing our job, which is strengthening ourselves.

Joy, when you compare yourself with others and let these comparisons disappoint you, you build a prison around you. You keep your self-worth caged in this prison. When you compare, you sabotage your self-worth. You feel insecure and intimidated in other people's presence. These insecurities keep you stuck. You don't lose yourself to others; you lose to your own insecurities.

Think about this for a moment. Michael Jordan did not have muscles like Arnold Schwarzenegger. Bill Gates did not chase Einstein's intelligence. Bruce Lee never wanted to build Disneyland. But they were all happy and successful, and built a legacy for the next generation."

Master paused for a while and then asked, "What do you think made them build a legacy?"

Master then explained, "The reason is simple. They did what they could with everything they had. They didn't compare or complain about what they didn't have and feel insecure. They believed in their own potential and did everything possible with their potential. This is what helped them create a legacy and inspire billions. They valued their self-worth, which led them to create the net worth they have today."

I affirmed with a nod.

Master explained, "One of the habits that limit people's potential is comparison. This habit of comparison is self-sabotaging. When you compare, you view the world to be more important than yourself, and you do everything to accommodate the view of the world. When you believe that your worth is minimal in comparison to others, you disapprove yourself of all the greatness that is within you."

Master continued, "Joy, did you notice that a lot of time people compare their weaknesses with others' strengths and not their strengths with others' strengths? Isn't that true?"

"Well, I never thought of it that way."

Master continued, "High achievers know and embrace the fact that each of us have strengths, and each of us have areas that need improvement. That's what makes us unique. They appreciate themselves as well as the differences each of us possess. They never feel threatened or insecure. Every time they find someone more talented and stronger than them, they wear the learner's hat. They don't compare and weigh themselves down; they appreciate and value everyone's worth. When you compare, you assess your self-worth outside-in, but high achievers approach their self-worth inside-out.

Let us assume that you meet someone who is extremely good at running. He has run five marathons in the last six months and knows what it takes to run a marathon. You are preparing to run a marathon in the next two months. Now, you have two choices. You can compare yourself with him and feel threatened, or ask him how he prepared and learn from him. The choice is always yours.

When it comes to the success of your career or business, it is just the same. Most people never earn beyond a certain level of income because they continue to compare and lower their self-worth. This low self-worth makes them feel intimidated and stops them from learning from other successful people. They forget the fact that it is learning that increases earning."

All my life, I compared myself with others and sabotaged my self-worth. Every time I thought of starting my entrepreneurship journey, I compared myself with those who have accomplished a lot and felt unworthy. I often felt that I lacked the required skills, knowledge, and money to be a successful entrepreneur. I was always thinking about others' strengths more than my own strengths. I was living in the prison of comparison.

It is time for me to break out of this prison and trust my potential and value my self-worth. I now know that I don't have to compare myself with others and think that others are exceptions. All I needed is to acknowledge that others are just an example of what is possible.

I must focus on learning from everyone, which is the key to develop my self-worth and my net worth.

Inspiration Corner

It was her turn now. The wait for her had been long. It had been the longest day of her life, and there came the announcement, "Contestant number 43212."

She walked on to the stage of **Britain's Got Talent, Season 3**. *She was not very beautifully dressed, or worried about the fact that she was about to face the most critical judges of the show. She was also not really anxious about being watched across the globe.*

There she was, facing a large hall full of audience, most of them half her age.

One of the judges asked, "What's your name, lady?"

"Susan Boyle" came the response.

The judge asked, "Where are you from?"

She fumbled and fumbled again before she could complete her response; one could hear the audience booing, and the judges nodding their heads in despair.

The next judge asked, "How old are you?"

"I am 47," she said. After a long pause, filled with booing and laughter from the audience, she said, "That's just one side of it." Her statement raised the eyebrows of the judges and a few others in the hall. After all, she looked very plain and had just made a statement that was probably the opposite of what she looked. And she also sounded a little overconfident.

She said, "I am trying to be a professional singer and want to be as successful as Elaine Paige."

(Elaine Paige is an English singer and actress best known for her work in musical theater)

The judges smiled, and she was nearly ridiculed by the audience.

Everyone had built a perception based on Susan's plain, homely appearance and contrasting high aspirations.

Fighting all odds was Susan. Very few knew that she was diagnosed with learning difficulties. Susan had had a difficult childhood and had been bullied as a child. She had been nicknamed 'Susie Simple' in school.

Susan's first performance, I Dreamed a Dream, was widely reported, and millions of people viewed the video on YouTube. Elaine Paige (Susan's role model) called her "a role model for everyone who has a dream."

The rest was history!

Susan became one of the most famous singers ever. Her journey to stardom started only at the age of 47, and it is still on. But the wait had been really long.

Susan, after her success, said, "Modern society is too quick to judge people on their appearances. There is not much you can do about it; it is the way they think, it is the way they are. But maybe this could teach them a lesson, or set an example."

She also said, "I know what they were thinking, but why should it matter as long as I can sing?"

Truth #4: Winners do quit, and quitters do win!

As we continued walking, I noticed that this place looked very beautiful and mystical during the early morning hours. We were so deeply engrossed in the conversation that we did not realize that we had walked too far. We decided to walk back and continued our discussion about high achievers.

Master asked, "Have you ever heard of the phrase 'winners don't quit, and quitters don't win'?"

"Yes, I have heard this saying several times while I was growing up. I believed in this so much that I persisted hard to achieve everything. The more challenges I faced, the more I persisted and refused to quit. But it only made me tired, angry, and anxious," I expressed my anguish to Master.

Master replied, "Yes, it is important to persist and not give up. However, the truth is, there are times when you need to give up, and you must quit. All high achievers know when to quit and when to persist. A lot of people do not quit because they equate quitting with weakness. They think, 'If I quit, I am not good enough or capable enough.'"

I was patiently listening to this insight.

"Most people do not want to believe that sometimes quitting is essential; letting go is essential. When you do not understand this, you actually fall into a trap and end up fighting the wrong battles. Joy, do you know what is worse than moving in the wrong direction?"

I waited for Master to share the answer.

"It is moving in the wrong direction enthusiastically," Master said, and we laughed. "When you don't quit, you are often heading in the wrong direction enthusiastically, and that can lead you nowhere."

"Imagine someone who does not like the job and does not quit the job either. All he does is curse the nature of the job and criticize the people he is working with every day. He then complains and says, 'My talent is not fully utilized.' When you ask him, 'Why don't you quit?' he would say, 'I think I am settled in this job and quitting is too much of a hassle.' Well, this is what everyone does. When people don't quit, they settle. They settle for something lesser than their potential. Quitting is necessary for your growth; settling is the thing that you should be worried about. For instance, quitting a job you don't enjoy is necessary; settling in a job that doesn't serve you is what you should be worried about. Only when you quit, you allow space for other things to be created in life."

> *If you never quit anything, you're going to have less time for the things that really matter*
> *~ Eric Barker*

"Can you give me more examples of this, Master?"

"Sure. For example, you must know when to quit the business idea that's not giving you the returns you want. You must quit investing your time on a specific client who is not allowing you the space to grow. If you continue to invest in a business idea or a client that doesn't serve you, you will end up facing hardships."

"How do I determine when to quit?"

"There are two situations when you must quit. First, when your investment does not fetch you the right results you want. It's that simple. The investment need not necessarily be monetary; it could be your energy and efforts as well. Second, when there is change, and it demands you to quit the old and embrace the new."

"What makes quitting easy for high achievers?"

"It's because high achievers have faith in what is going to unfold. They quit because they are driven by faith; they know that if they don't quit, they will settle for anything. Settling is driven by fear. So, the next time you think of quitting, let your faith be bigger than your fear. Remember, it is important to quit at times, and winners do quit, and quitters do win!"

"Master, quitting allows us to redirect our potential onto the right path, and if not, we end up exerting all our energy on the wrong path. Quitting is important, and quitting at the right time is more important. I am more aware of the importance of quitting now. I am ready to own this truth."

Inspiration Corner

There was a village that was infested with monkeys. There were so many monkeys that it started to cause problems to the local villagers and farmers. The monkeys began to steal food from the people and fruits from the trees. It got so bad that something had to be done. That's when a wise man stepped up and said to the community, "I've got a plan."

He drilled a tiny hole on the side of a coconut and drained out the coconut water. The hole was big enough for the monkey's hand to go in but too small for a monkey's fist to come out. He then filled a third of it with peanuts and placed it near the trees that the monkeys frequently visited.

A monkey figured out that there were peanuts inside the coconut, so he stuck his tiny hand in there and grabbed a handful of peanuts. The plan worked, and his fist did not come out.

The monkey would not let go of the peanuts. The monkey did not see that he could let go and free his other hand and climb away. When the villagers saw that the monkey's hand was stuck in the coconut, they chased and caught the monkey.

The only thing that the monkey had to do was quit on the peanuts and let himself free.

Truth #5: Perfection is the path to mediocrity

We returned from our walk and decided to meet in Master's study room after an hour.

As I reached Master's room, one of the helpers came to us and served us coffee. We continued our conversation while sipping our coffees.

I waited for Master to share more of his pearls of wisdom.

Master said, "Joy, did you ever wait for the perfect moment to start something?"

"Yes, I have, and the perfect moment never arrived," I replied with a smile.

"Joy, perfection leads you on the path of mediocrity. Yes, that's the truth. The more you wait for the perfect time, perfect place, or anything perfect, the more you delay your progress. When you delay your progress, you never reach your potential. The truth is, waiting for perfection sucks the energy out of you and paralyzes your ability to act. High achievers know that perfection is a myth, and it only leads you to mediocrity."

"I often meet individuals who are unwilling to start a business because they want the perfect moment or a perfect plan in hand. There are many who do not want to get into a relationship as they are searching for the 'perfect' partner. There are endless examples of such perfection traps that people get caught in."

"What do high achievers do to stay away from this trap?" I enquired.

"First, they know that perfection is the monster that kills their progress. They own this truth. Second, they stay focused on making progress by taking action. Joy, you must constantly assess and check if you are getting caught up in the need for perfection. If you find yourself stuck in this need, take action immediately."

I said, "That's an amazing idea! Irrespective of whether the action gives me the result or not, I must be willing to take action. I will at least be making progress than being stuck."

"You are right, Joy."

Perfectionism is not the same thing as striving for excellence. Perfection is not about healthy achievement and growth.

Perfectionism is the belief that if we live perfect, look perfect, and act perfect, we can minimize or avoid the pain of blame, judgment, and shame. It's a shield. Perfectionism is a twenty-ton shield that we lug around, thinking it will protect us, when, in fact, it's the thing that's really preventing us from being seen and taking flight.

Perfectionism is not self-improvement. Perfectionism is, at its core, about trying to earn approval and acceptance.

Most perfectionists were raised being praised for achievement and performance (grades, manners, rule-following habit, people-pleasing nature, appearance, sports). Somewhere along the way, we adopt this dangerous and debilitating belief system: I am what I accomplish and how well I accomplish it. Please. Perform. Perfect. Prove.

Healthy striving is self-focused—How can I improve? Perfectionism is other-focused—What will people think? Lay down the shield. Pick up your life.

~ Berne Brown

As I introspected, I recognized that I had been trying to do too much, too well, and too right, for too long, thereby putting too much pressure on myself. I ended up creating too much stress. Chasing perfection had stopped me from making progress. It was time for me to break through this by owning this truth.

We were so involved in the conversation that we did not realize that it was afternoon. We decided to have lunch.

I noticed that many people had assembled in the hall for lunch. This was the tradition. Everyone would gather for breakfast, lunch, and dinner at specific times.

They all were discussing about the trek that was scheduled the next day morning. I could feel everyone's excitement. I was curious as well as concerned because I had never ever trekked before. After a few conversations with others, I saw Master. I went and sat next to him.

He said, "Joy, tomorrow we will be going on a trek to the nearby mountain. Do you want to join us?"

With a lot of hesitation, I agreed to join the trek.

Which truth should you accept?

o   Truth #1: Problems come to refine us not define us
✓   _____
✓   _____

o   Truth #2: Your Choices Shape Your Life
✓   _____
✓   _____

o   Truth #3: Your Self-Worth Defines Your Net worth
✓   _____
✓   _____

o   Truth #4: Winners do quit, and quitters do win!
✓   _____
✓   _____

o   Truth #5: Perfection is the path to mediocrity
✓   _____
✓   _____

PART 3

CHAPTER 6

DISCOVERING THE INVISIBLE CODE

The next day morning, we all gathered early to start our trek.

While on the trek, there were moments when I felt like quitting and walking back. But then I was reminded of the truths that I had committed to. I was determined to reach the top.

While trekking through the mountain, I was thinking of all the wisdom that Master had shared. What he had said until then had challenged my perspective. Every conversation I had had with Master helped me expand my self-awareness.

I started imagining how these lessons would help me live a life of deeper meaning and fulfillment.

I was confident that everything that I had learned would help me rise to the next level in my life. We took around three hours to reach the top of the mountain.

The view from the top was mesmerizing. This was the first time I had trekked, and this was the first time I saw the world from the top of a mountain. The cold breeze, the deep silence, and the mystic view were an experience of a lifetime. I was reminded of the quote, "The best view comes from the hardest climb."

"The best view comes from the hardest climb."

We were amidst many beautiful mountains. Everyone was enjoying the view. I noticed that Master was sitting next to a small tree and enjoying the silence. I sat next to him. After a while, Master asked, "Joy, today is going to be an important day of learning. Are you geared up, or are you tired?"

"I was waiting to know what else was going to unfold," I said, "How can I miss any opportunity to learn from you, Master?"

"We have heard of achievers who started their journey of achieving big aspirations with nothing. Today many of them live a wealthy and luxurious lifestyle; they have a family that's caring and loving. Many have earned a room full of awards and accolades and a lot more. In addition to having an achievers mindset, do you think that all achievers have something more?" asked Master.

"Maybe there is a secret code they know. But what about the people who do not have an achievers mindset?"

Master laughed at my statement and asked, "What will you do if you get to know the secret code? Also, what if I share with you ways to change your mindset?"

I was speechless for a moment and said, "If I know the secret code, I will certainly implement it in my life. I will certainly change my mindset as well."

"Okay, Joy. Let me tell you a story first."

Master was a great storyteller, and he had one story for every message he wanted to convey.

***

A businessman was in debt. His creditors were pressing him, and suppliers were demanding payment. He couldn't figure any way out. One day, he was sitting on a bench in the park with his head down, thinking about what could save the company from bankruptcy.

Suddenly, an old man appeared in front of him.

"I see that something is bothering you," he said. After listening to the businessman, the old man said, "I think I can help you."

He asked the businessman what his name was, wrote him a check, and said, "Take this money. We will meet again exactly one year from now, and you will be able to return the money to me at that time."

After that, he turned around and disappeared just as suddenly as he appeared. The businessman saw a check in his hands for an amount of 500 thousand dollars, signed by John Rockefeller, one of the wealthiest people in the world at that time!

"I could end all my problems in no time!" he thought. But instead, the businessman decided to put the check in a safe. The thought about the check gave him the strength to find a solution to save his business.

With the return of his optimism, he concluded profitable deals. He was more disciplined and made changes to the way he did business. During the next couple of months, he got out of debt and started to earn money again. He doubled his business in no time.

Exactly one year later, he returned to the park with the same check. At the agreed time, the old man appeared again. And at the moment, when the businessman wanted to return the check and share his story of success, a nurse ran up and grabbed the old man.

"I'm so glad I caught him!" she exclaimed, "I hope he wasn't bothering you. He always runs away from the house and tells everyone that he is John Rockefeller."

The businessman was amused. During the whole year, he was spinning and building a business, buying and selling, convinced that he had half a million dollars. He now wondered what gave him the strength and made him achieve everything.

***

"Joy, the story I shared is of every person who is stuck and has lost hope. The businessman was unaware of what made him achieve the new level of success. But the truth is, there was an invisible force guiding him to move forward. Most of us are unaware of this force.

I have always been fascinated to know and study this invisible force. I decoded this force, and today, I am going to share everything that I know about this powerful force."

"What could this force be?" I thought and was eagerly waiting to know.

"I call this 'the one invisible code'. It governs every result of your life. This powerful and simple code is practiced by all high achievers, elite athletes, global leaders, and successful entrepreneurs."

Master emphasized the words 'powerful' and 'simple'. I had noticed that many leaders like Richard Branson, Mark Zuckerberg, Ratan Tata, M. S. Dhoni, Sachin Tendulkar, Satya Nadella, and others always advocated one thing: the practice of simplicity. I was reminded of what Richard Branson said, "Complexity is your enemy. Any fool can make something complicated. It is hard to keep things simple."

The One Invisible Code

"Joy, your aspiration is the birthplace of all the greatness you can achieve; everything starts with having an aspiration. Whether it is Elon Musk's mission of SpaceX or Mark Zuckerberg's mission of connecting a billion people online, it is apparent that every great entrepreneur or successful leader begins their journey with an aspiration."

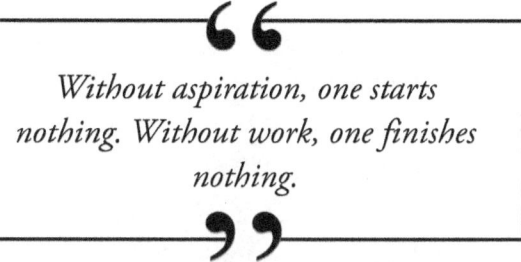

> *Without aspiration, one starts nothing. Without work, one finishes nothing.*

I asked, "Master, is it about setting bigger goals? There is so much spoken about goals. There are so many who set goals, but then when we really take an account, very few accomplish the goals they set. I am one such person who sets goals and ends up missing them always. And a lot of times, even after accomplishing the goals, I feel a vacuum and feel unfulfilled. I have seen individuals, teams, and organizations struggle to set goals and then decide to give up their goals midway."

"Joy, aspirations are not just about setting a bigger goal; goals often lack the fuel to ignite action. The fuel that ignites an action is emotion. Emotions are the reason why you feel inspired to take consistent action. Goals are backed by logic, whereas aspirations are backed by deep emotions as well as logic. Goals give you short-term motivation, whereas aspirations inspire you in the long run. It is emotion that gives you reasons to raise the bar and make a difference."

"Master, I have read that logic is usually the left side of the brain, and emotion is the right side of the brain. So, are you saying that goals are logical and stimulate only the left side of the brain, while aspirations stimulate both the right as well as the left side of the brain?"

> *Logic will get you from A to B.*
> *Imagination will take you everywhere.*
> *~ Albert Einstein*

"You are right, Joy. Most goal-setting systems engage only at the logical level. But the fact is 80% of our life is driven by our emotions and only 20% by logic. Now imagine, what would be the result of setting a goal that only stimulates logic and not emotions? When you decode the lives of successful entrepreneurs, corporate leaders, change-makers, and high achievers, you will know that they all believe in aspirations. They understand that setting a goal is a systematic and logical process while fulfilling aspirations is a systematic, logical, and emotional process. That's why successful people are committed to aspirations."

I said, "This is interesting! So, when I am not emotionally committed, I will not take action, or I will take inconsistent action. I might set goals but not achieve them. Even if I achieve them, I may never feel fulfilled and never feel driven to achieve the next level of success that I deserve."

"Let's talk about the traditional goal-setting system. You must have heard of the SMART goal-setting process. Have you, Joy?"

"Yes, Master, I have always set goals in a SMART way."

"SMART goal-setting is an amazing system to set goals. It is a very logical and systematic way of setting goals, and it helps you set Specific, Measurable, Actionable, Relevant, and Time-bound goals. But did you notice that the element of emotion is missing from this system?

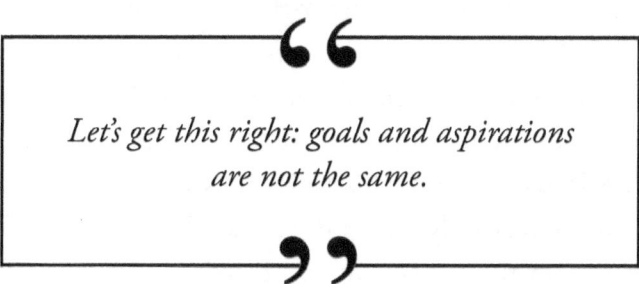

Let's get this right: goals and aspirations are not the same.

Let me explain this with an example: When you set a SMART goal, you would probably state something like this: *I want to start a real-estate consulting business in Mumbai by December 2020 and make a profit of Rs 25 crore in the first six months.* Now, the question is, where do you find emotion in this? Why do you want to achieve this goal? What's the emotion that will drive you to strive harder?"

Now when I think of it, I had no choice but to agree with Master.

Master continued, "When you set SMART goals, you end up exerting a lot of time and energy in the process, but you never feel inspired to take action. Emotions are the reason why you strive hard, remain focused, and endure all the pain while facing challenges. When you are emotionally invested, you don't give up even during testing times.

The most common mistake people commit while setting goals is taking emotions out of the equation. And then they wonder why they are unable to achieve their goals or why they are unfulfilled even after achieving their goals."

I agreed with Master.

"Joy, emotion is often referred to as energy in motion (e-motion). When you find yourself stuck or unfulfilled, it is because you are not emotionally involved in the process of setting and achieving goals. Your energy is stuck in things that are least important to you.

When you deconstruct the life of great leaders and high achievers, you will discover that the thing that differentiates them is their ability to be driven by emotions and not just by logic. Think of Martin Luther King Jr, when he stood for his people. He was deeply moved by emotions and not by any systematic and logical goal. In the end, he was assassinated. Had he been logical, he would not have fought the battle against slavery. Similarly, Steve Jobs could fulfill his aspirations and revolutionize the world of personal computers only because he was deeply driven by emotion. Emotions were also the driving force behind Mother Teresa's service to people. It was Sachin Tendulkar's emotions that gave him the strength to serve the Indian cricket team for close to 24 years."

I responded enthusiastically, "This is amazing, Master! Setting SMART goals is not enough, but being emotionally involved is the key to feeling fulfilled."

Now, I was more curious and wanted to learn everything about aspirations. *How do I set the right kind of aspirations? How can I practice it every day? How do I know if I am on the right track while setting aspirations? How do I know if what I am setting is an aspiration and not a goal?*

Master was happy to see me excited. He always liked my enthusiasm to enquire and learn more. We started discussing and delving deeper into understanding the first step of the one invisible code—aspiration.

"Joy, aspiration is the invisible force that guides you to your destiny. When you start living your aspiration, you become who you are meant to be. You become an unstoppable force.."

After the insightful conversation, we started back from our trek, and by the time we reached home, it was evening. Master said, "Let us meet in an hour, Joy. I am sure you must now be thinking of how to set the right aspirations. I have an answer to your question."

By now, Master knew what my next question would be. We exchanged smiles, decided to meet in an hour, and walked back to our rooms.

CHAPTER 7

THE ASPIRATIONS – KNOWING THE GAPP

GAPP Framework

We met after an hour, and Master shared with me the GAPP framework. He said, "Aspirations are future-focused, emotionally-driven, and positively-crafted. GAPP is a system that helps you in setting aspirations."

I started making notes.

Step #1: Be Grateful

"Joy, being grateful makes you graceful! The first step to set the right aspirations is to be grateful for what you already have. This enables you to tap into an achievers mindset. When you complain, compare, criticize, and are ungrateful, you set reactive aspirations, and you seldom succeed. When you focus on what you have and not what you don't have, you operate from the feeling of 'I am enough' and not from the feeling of 'I lack'. When you are setting aspirations from the space of 'lack', it seldom helps you succeed.

> *Being grateful makes you graceful!*
> *~ Sharat Sharma*

Gratitude opens your heart to endless possibilities and lets you experience a state of flow—a state where you are completely immersed and experience the least resistance. When you are grateful, you notice simple pleasures and acknowledge them. This makes you happier and more resilient. Being grateful also strengthens your relationship with yourself and others. You are less critical and don't pay attention to the voice between your ears which hinders your growth. When you are grateful, it improves your health and reduces stress too. This allows you to unleash your full potential. When you are grateful, you are anchored in the present moment. You realize that everything is fine just the way it is. Gratitude also helps you stop fighting, resisting, controlling, and chasing pleasure. The first step is to decide what you are grateful for, in every significant aspect of your life."

Step #2: Defining Aspirations

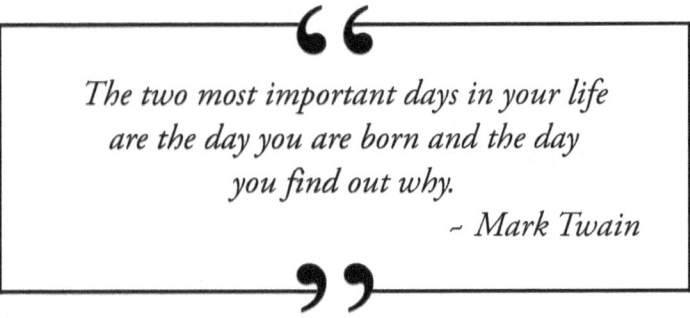

The two most important days in your life are the day you are born and the day you find out why.
~ Mark Twain

"Most people think of income as their ultimate goal. They want to influence a lot of people, and they are least committed to the impact they must create. Thinking of income first and impact last is the biggest mistake that most people commit."

"Why do you say that, Master?" I asked inquisitively.

"Joy, have you heard of people who are successful yet unfulfilled? These are the people who have money but have lost freedom; they have luxury but have forgotten laughter. In spite of achieving a lot, everything feels shallow. All this is because they chase income first."

"Got it!"

"If your first focus is only income, you will soon be demotivated. Chasing money alone limits you from creating the big impact that's possible."

"What's the alternative, Master?"

"Joy, all high achievers think of the impact they want to create first. Focusing on the impact results in expanding their influence, and the income follows. So, now deliberate and think about the impact you want to create, the influence you want to have, and the income you want to generate."

"This is going to be a tough exercise, Master."

"Let me help you with this, Joy. When you are thinking of impact, you are driven by a strong desire to serve and make a difference. You are looking for meaning in the work that you do and not the activities that you need to perform. You know, in order to deserve more, you need to first serve more. Impact comes from not *what* you do; it comes from *why* you do things. Your 'why' gives you meaning and purpose. To find your 'why', you must constantly introspect and ask yourself if everything that you do is making a difference and adding value."

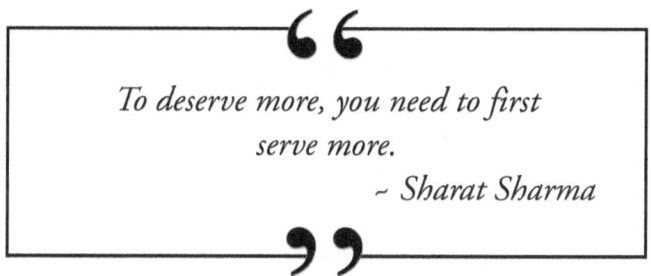

> *To deserve more, you need to first serve more.*
> *~ Sharat Sharma*

Knowing the emotion that drives you – What is your 'WHY'?

Master continued to explain, "Your 'why' is your motivation. It is the reason you wake up feeling inspired each day and the reason you go to sleep peacefully. It drives you to persist even during a phase of adversity. Knowing your 'why'—the emotion behind your goal—turns your goals into meaningful aspirations. Initially, your goal could be making more money, buying a house, or looking good. However, when you dig deep and become aware of the real source of motivation, your 'why', you will be inspired to take action.

Your 'why' comes from within and is not influenced by anything that's outside. That's why it acts as an intrinsic motivator. Once you discover your 'why', you don't need someone to remind you or motivate you."

"How do I find my why?" I asked.

"Let me give you the steps to identify your 'why'. Be sure to write a response to every question."

Steps to identify your 'why'

Step 1: Write what your goal is.

Step 2: Ask why.

Step 3: Ask why until you get the intrinsic reason/motivation/drive.

Step 4: Once you find your intrinsic drive, ask yourself why you should do it, and how you would bring value.

Step 5: What will happen if you don't do it? What will happen to you and the others you want to serve?

Step 6: Now make this specific.

An example
- ❖ Write what your goal is (E.g., *I want to start a health food store.*)
- ❖ Ask why. Your answer might be: *I want to be an entrepreneur and not an employee. This will help me make a lot of money.*
- ❖ Ask why again - *so that I can empower families to make the right choices while selecting their food.*
- ❖ Ask why again - *so that the families can live a healthy, happy, and fulfilled life.*

- ❖ Why? What will happen if you help more people lead a healthy and happy life? *I will feel fulfilled and know that I am living up to my potential and creating an impact on the way people pursue healthy eating.*
- ❖ Then ask these: Why should I do it? What will happen to the people I want to help if I don't do it? The answer could be: *I don't want to just make money, but I genuinely care. I know families suffer because they don't eat healthily, and in some cases, they don't know where to find healthy eating options. If I don't do it, families will continue to suffer, and this will be painful.*
- ❖ Can you make this specific? *Help one lakh families in the next 12 months.*

"Your 'why' could be: Empower one lakh families to make healthy eating choices and enjoy worry-free living.

The key is to continue asking 'why' until you arrive at your ultimate reason for pursuing your goal. Initially, your reason might be money, but then the more you ask, the more you will know that the deeper reason is the impact you wish to create. This reason is the fuel that will ignite you to go the extra mile every time you feel like giving up. You must constantly remind yourself of what will happen if you don't do this."

"I understand this, Master."

"Joy, let's go deeper.

Let us break the 'why' statement: Empower one lakh families to make healthy eating choices and enjoy worry-free living. You will notice that it has a few elements: Who are you serving? How are you serving them? What impact do you want to leave?

Joy, while a lot of times income is driven by a selfish mindset, the impact is driven by a service mindset, and that's the game-changer. To make sure you are aligned with these aspirations, you must ask a few more questions."

Steps to identify your 'why'

Step 1 : Write what your goal is.

Step 2 : Ask why.

Step 3 : Ask why until you get the intrinsic reason/motivation/drive.

Step 4 : Once you find your intrinsic drive, ask yourself why you should do it, and how you would bring value.

Step 5 : What will happen if you don't do it? What will happen to you and the others you want to serve?

Step 6 : Now make this specific.

Questions you must ask

- Does this 'why' move me emotionally? Does this make me happy?
- Do I see myself doing this for the rest of my life, even if things get tough?
- Am I willing to persevere even when I don't see results in the short-term?
- If I do this for the rest of my life, will the impact that I create be felt even after I am gone? Will the work that I do be read as part of my eulogy?

"These are powerful questions, Master."

"Once you are clear with the IMPACT, the next step is to think of the INFLUENCE. To fulfill your impact, you must also work on multiplying your influence. There are two areas that you must work on to multiply your influence: Growth and relationships."

Growth

- What are the things that you must learn continuously to grow personally and professionally?
- What are the experiences that will help you grow?

Relationships

- Who are the mentors that I must connect with? (mentors, influencers, support group)
- Who are the people I must support?

"Having a powerful IMPACT statement and INFLUENCE results in your INCOME. As the last step, define how much wealth you want to create. This will help you design your strategies as you begin your journey," said Master.

"I was confused initially and felt this would be complex. With these steps, you have simplified the process to define my Impact, Influence, and Income. You have always simplified things, Master," I said and thanked him.

Step #3: Being Progress-Centric Actions

"The next step is to make your aspirations progress-centric. You do this by setting smaller milestones. These milestones act as indicators and guide you in the right direction. They also help you make the necessary course correction. You can create a roadmap of milestones by quantifying your aspirations with timelines and tangible actions. When your aspirations are progress-centric, you eliminate every possibility of getting influenced by external distractions. To make your aspirations progress-centric, you must set smaller, specific, time-bound actions."

Steps to set progress-centric aspirations

1) **Make them smaller:** To make progress, chunk down the bigger aspirations. Write the smaller parts you wish to accomplish.
2) **Specific:** Specificity brings clarity to the mind and helps you focus. Make small specific chunks you want to achieve.
3) **Time-bound:** Allocate timelines to the smaller parts. This helps you in prioritizing and planning. Allocate time to the smaller specific parts identified in the previous step.
4) **Actions:** List down the actions that will lead you to complete the smaller chunks. List down every action that will enable you to fulfill these smaller, specific, time-bound parts.

"Well, this is more about converting our aspirations into actions. Am I right, Master?"

"Yes, Joy, and there is one final step to complete the GAPP framework. It is about setting the priorities right."

Step #4: Setting The Priorities Right

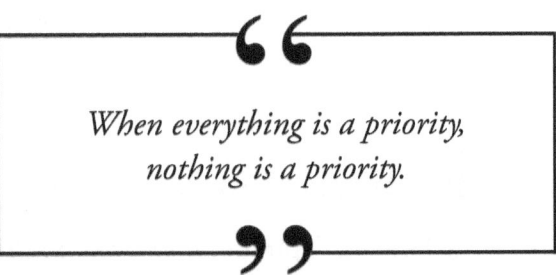

When everything is a priority, nothing is a priority.

"Most people feel overwhelmed because they consider everything a priority. Setting the priorities right is the most important step in fulfilling your aspirations. When you don't set the priorities right, you end up doing unimportant things."

"How do I prioritize right?"

"From the previous step, you have the smaller, specific, time-bound actions that you must take. Now, all these actions can be divided into three categories."

The three categories of actions

1) **High impact**

   In the book, *The One Thing*, authors Gary Keller and Jay Papasan say that one way to create a clear priority is by asking questions. They recommend asking this powerful question: What's the ONE thing I can do such that by doing it everything else will be easier or unnecessary? This is a great way to determine high-impact activities.

2) **Medium impact**

   To identify things that have a medium impact, think of the actions that must be done not immediately but eventually.

3) **Low impact**

   Low-impact activities are activities that do not hold much significance and do not contribute immediately to your aspirations. These are nice-to-do-activities but they may not add much value. You may eliminate these activities or even delegate these activities to others.

"Joy, this is the first step of the invisible code—setting the right aspirations using the GAPP framework."

This framework was insightful and meaningful, and I was fully engaged in it. More importantly, it made me think. I made notes and reflected on every step that Master had shared. Today was one of the longest days, and Master had rightly said that this was an important day.

It was very late, and we both decided to call it a day and continue our conversation the next day.

I was thrilled to have learned about the GAPP framework.

The GAPP Framework

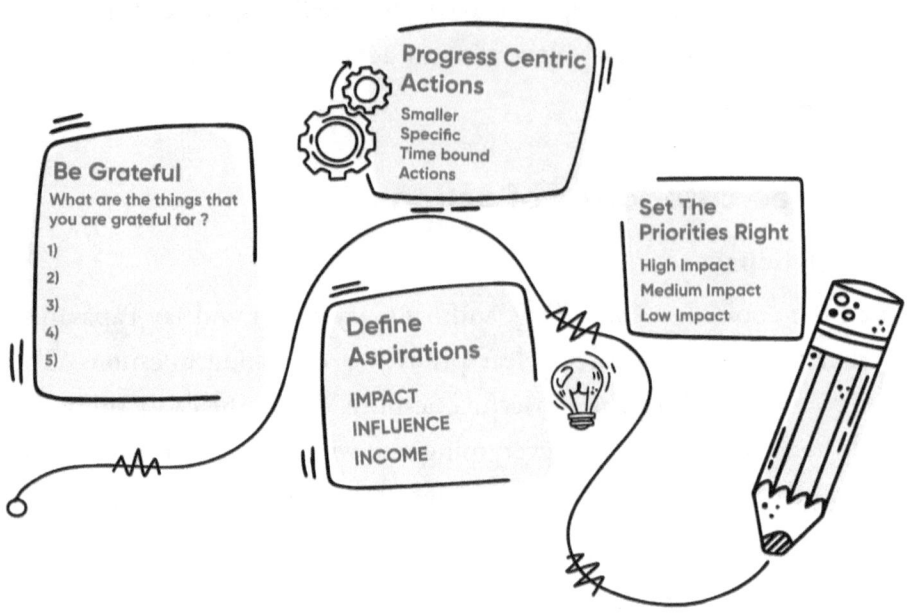

Be Grateful	Define Aspirations	Progress Centric Actions	Set The Priorities Right
What are things that you are grateful of?	IMPACT:	Smaller:	High Impact:
	INFLUENCE:	Specific:	Medium Impact:
	INCOME:	Time Bound:	Low Impact:
		Actions:	

CHAPTER 8

THE BELIEFS – BREAKING THE BOUNDARIES

The next day when I woke up, I felt pain in my muscles. They were sore after the trek. I quickly got ready for the day and rushed to have breakfast. As always, many others had surrounded Master. They were all engaged in a conversation with Master.

I greeted Master. In spite of the long trek and tiring day, Master looked as fresh as a daisy. I noticed that the conversation was about beliefs.

I heard Master say, "Our beliefs are our boundaries. We must break them often."

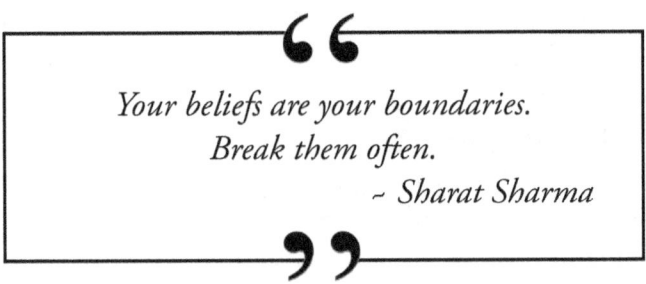

*Your beliefs are your boundaries.
Break them often.
~ Sharat Sharma*

Someone asked Master, "So, how do we know our beliefs, and how can we break them?"

I was listening to the conversation.

"There are two levels of beliefs that all of us must possess. One is to believe in our aspirations.

While everyone waits until the world believes in their aspirations, every achiever believes in their aspirations, much before the world believes in them. That's the first level of belief -'believing in one's aspirations'."

"The reason why most people don't believe in their aspirations is because of the beliefs they have about themselves. That's the second level of belief. There are many non-supportive beliefs that we hold on to which stops us from achieving our aspirations.

The fact is a lot of times you win or lose the battle much before you even fight the battle because of the non-supportive beliefs you hold.

Every great achiever has a set of core beliefs that shapes their life. These beliefs act as a guide and give us directions. During challenging times, those who do not have supportive beliefs alter their aspirations and match them with their beliefs. But those who have stronger aspirations work on refining their non-supportive beliefs.

For example, you want to start a business, but then you hold yourself back and never start a business because you think you don't have enough experience. You want to be promoted at your job, but then you believe that you do not have great oratory skills. All these non-supportive beliefs stop you from pursuing your aspirations."

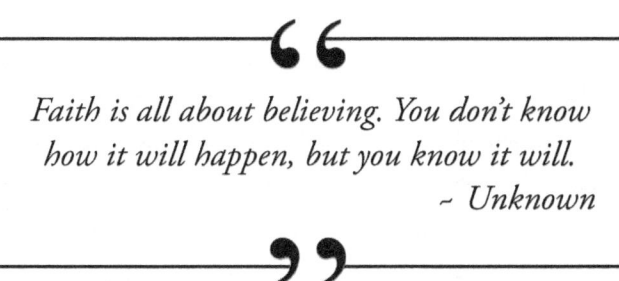

> *Faith is all about believing. You don't know how it will happen, but you know it will.*
> *~ Unknown*

Some of the non-supportive beliefs that we hold on to and suffer

- ❖ This is not the right time.
- ❖ I don't have the required skills.
- ❖ I am too old.
- ❖ I am too young.
- ❖ I have too many things on my plate.
- ❖ It's too risky.
- ❖ I don't know the right people.
- ❖ I am not capable enough.
- ❖ I am too tired; I deserve a break.
- ❖ I don't have the perfect plan.
- ❖ I am comfortable doing just this.
- ❖ I need an original idea.
- ❖ I don't have enough money.
- ❖ I am not credible enough.

"Beliefs are like the engines that drive our experiences. If the engine is outdated or does not support the vehicle, it is important for us to change

The 'One' Invisible Code

or upgrade the engine. Only this ensures that the engine performs at the optimum level. Similarly, we must renew our beliefs to reach our full potential. If not, these beliefs create inertia and keep us stuck. So, let me tell you a story to explain this."

There was a small village that was known for its happy people. All the villagers worked hard together, celebrated festivals together, and supported each other. As a ritual, all the villagers stored all their crops in a storehouse they had built. Anyone who wanted anything could go into the storehouse and take what they wanted. This helped create equality among the villagers and a feeling of togetherness. This storehouse also helped them in the non-farming season.

One day, someone spread a rumor in the village that the storehouse was haunted. From that day, no one dared to go inside the storehouse. In spite of having everything in the storehouse, they could not even have a single meal a day. They became extremely unhappy. It was not the farming season, and they had no option but to live in misery. Many of the elders in the village went to the neighboring villages asking for help, but they returned empty-handed. Days and weeks passed with not much respite. As time passed, many started to blame their fate and cursed the misfortune that the villagers had to experience.

One day, all the children in the village were playing right outside the storehouse. While they were playing, the ball accidentally fell inside the storehouse. Knowing the fact that the house was haunted, all the children ran away. While all the children ran in one direction, Raja, the youngest child, who did not know anything about the house being haunted, ran into the storehouse.

The other children went to the villagers and narrated the incident. The villagers, including Raja's mother, started looking for Raja. They screamed and shouted for Raja while standing outside the storehouse.

Raja was searching for the ball inside the storehouse. He first looked to his left and then to his right. When he did not see the ball, he went further inside. Finally, he spotted the ball. Just then, he heard the villagers screaming his name. He heard his mother. As he started to pick the ball, he noticed a shiny object next to it. He picked up the ball and the shiny object and ran outside.

The villagers were happy as well as shocked to see Raja. They never thought Raja would come back alive.

As soon as Raja's mother saw him, she cried and gave him a hug. Then she noticed that Raja was carrying a shiny object in his hand. Upon examining, she discovered that Raja was holding a piece of gold. All the villagers gathered around and asked Raja if he had seen more of this inside the storehouse.

Raja affirmed with a nod. When the villagers heard that there was more gold inside the storehouse, they gathered courage and went inside. They found that the storehouse was filled with bricks of gold. Soon, the village, which was living in poverty, became richer than ever before.

In spite of having all the wealth in their own village, the villagers had not accessed it. They believed that the storehouse was haunted. A mere rumor turned into a strong belief which kept the villagers away from their own food and all the treasure that was present.

Master explained, "Most of us are like the villagers. We do not access the treasure within us and deprive ourselves of our own potential by believing in the things that others tell us."

Everyone was listening to Master with complete attention.

"I want you all to take a moment and think about all the beliefs that you have unknowingly acquired."

As an inquisitive student, I asked, "Are we born with beliefs? Where did the beliefs come from? Can our beliefs be changed?"

Master responded, "I would like to read something that Rudolf Waltz wrote: To the as-yet-unborn, to all innocent wisps of undifferentiated nothingness: Watch out for life. I have caught life. I have come down with life. I was a wisp of undifferentiated nothingness, and then a little peephole opened quite suddenly. Light and sound poured in. Voices began to describe me and my surroundings. Nothing they said could be appealed. They said I was a boy named Rudolf Waltz, and that was that. They said the year was 1932, and that was that. They said I was in Midland City, Ohio, and that was that. They never shut up. Year after year, they piled detail upon detail. They do it still. Do you know what they say now? They say the year is 1982, and that I am 50 years old."

As Master finished reading, there was complete silence.

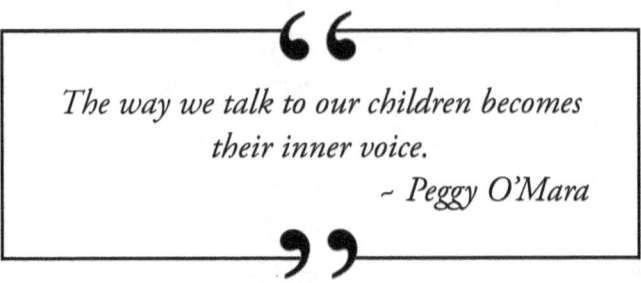

> *The way we talk to our children becomes their inner voice.*
> ~ Peggy O'Mara

What Master had shared was profound. It opened a flood of thoughts in my mind. I thought about how we are given labels as we are born, which turn into beliefs. Some of these beliefs empower us, but there are many that limit us too.

Master, "It is said that a newborn is a *tabula rasa*, which means that, at birth, the mind of a human is as blank as a plain sheet of paper. There are no preconceived ideas or predetermined beliefs. Our mind is a clean slate. But it is only for the first few seconds of our life. In these first few moments, the child is without beliefs and identity. The child is soon given a wristband with a number, gender, and a certificate of birth. Within days, the child is taught about the religion he or she would be following and the language that he or she would be speaking. The child is then told about the set of beliefs he or she must conform to in order to survive in the world."

Someone asked Master, "Are beliefs formed so easily? I mean, just by listening to things?"

"Not really, but everything that is said to you does have a lot of influence on how your beliefs are shaped. When some of these thoughts are repeated over and over again, the beliefs become powerful and stronger. They become your subconscious beliefs. In very less time, these beliefs shape the child's view of the world. The prospect to succeed or fail depends largely on these beliefs. The impressionable child starts to absorb the beliefs of others.

The beliefs of others become the beliefs of the child. The limitations of others become the limitations of the child. As a child, we had little or no ability to choose what is right and wrong for us.

Not only what we listen to, but what we see has a profound effect on our beliefs. While growing up, if we see things that are negative, they have an impact on our beliefs. Whether these beliefs are narrow or wide, empowering or disempowering, supportive or non-supportive, we did not question these beliefs."

One of the people asked, "Is that the reason why most of us imbibe the habits of our parents?"

"Yes, and as we grew up, every experience we had contributed to the way our beliefs shaped up. Our schooling, our peers, the movies we saw, the stories we heard, the heroes, and ideals we followed, all of these contributed to how we view the world today."

I asked, "Didn't we challenge any of them?"

"Unless you were a rebel, you did not challenge any of them. You adapted to others' ways of being and believing. These beliefs shaped your mindset of being a survivor, an explorer, a dreamer, or an achiever.

Let me give you an example. Imagine a person who goes through a rough childhood. As a child, he does not receive much love. While growing up, he constantly hears about relationships being painful. He sees his parents constantly arguing and then finally divorcing. As a teenager, he gets bullied by other children in the neighborhood. As a result, he chooses not to interact with others. As an adult, he gets rejected by the girl he dated for over two years. All these experiences shape his beliefs. He now believes that relationships don't work, and there is no point investing time in nurturing them. He starts to believe that staying aloof is a wiser choice than to trust someone and struggle in a relationship. This view shapes all of his relationships. He might struggle to find a life partner, business partner, or even strong relationships with fellow colleagues. He might find it difficult to build and nurture relationships unless he challenges his beliefs and finds ways to alter his limiting beliefs."

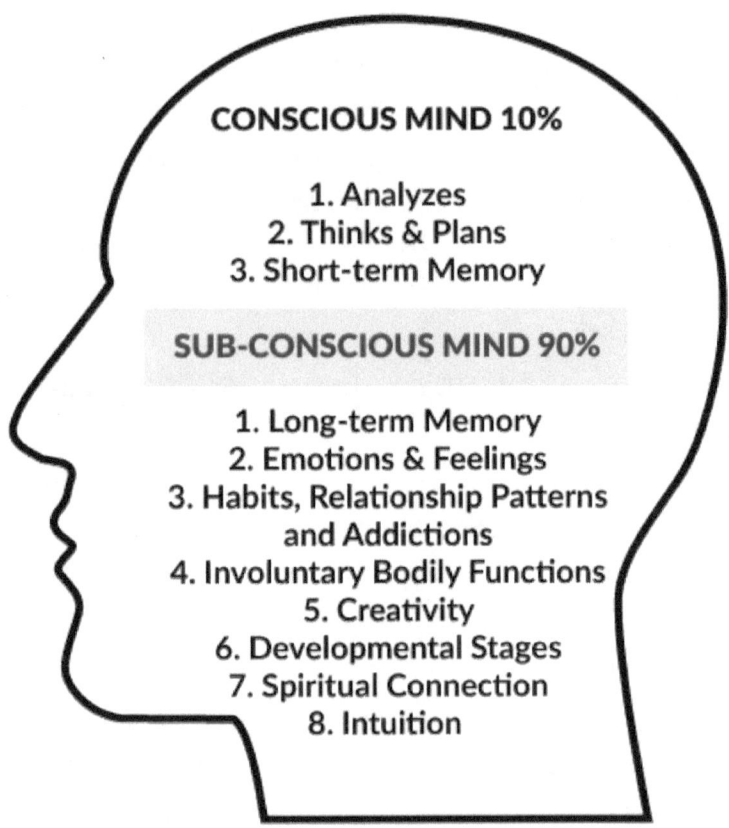

I agreed with Master. I was reminded of my childhood friend and how he would do small tasks like selling stationery during our school days. Taking risks came very naturally to him. He was from a business family and always wanted to start his own business. Everything he spoke and did was business-like. Now I understood that it was because of the beliefs he had developed while growing up.

I remember how his father would give us useful lessons in business. I did not bother to pay attention to it, but my friend would make the most of these lessons. We all knew that he would become a successful businessman someday, and he eventually became one. What amazed me the most was that he started his business while we were chasing degrees.

On the other end, while growing up, I only heard and believed that chasing degrees and getting a job would help me lead a better life. That was the race I was part of for the most part of my life. I followed what I believed I must follow, while my friend followed his beliefs.

Master continued sharing his words of wisdom, "The truth is, your beliefs affect every aspect of your life. It affects the way you see yourself, your health, your wealth, your work, your relationships, your aspirations, what is possible and what is not, what is right and what is wrong, what is important and what is not, what is good and what is evil, what is danger and what is safety, what is acceptable and what is unacceptable, etc."

"That's pretty much everything in life, Master!" someone exclaimed.

"Yes, without even realizing it, we run most part of our life based on these beliefs. Our beliefs, our mindset, or the way we see ourselves eventually end up dictating our entire life. In fact, at this very moment, whatever you have accomplished or failed to accomplish is because of the beliefs that you hold on to. Our beliefs expand or shrink the level of success we achieve. For you to achieve the next level of success, you must expand your beliefs."

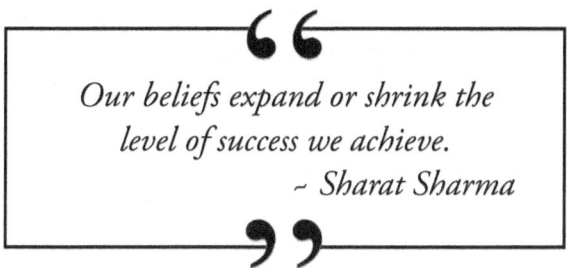

Our beliefs expand or shrink the level of success we achieve.
~ Sharat Sharma

"Our growth is determined by the positive beliefs that we have. And I must spend time challenging and changing my negative beliefs? Is that true, Master?"

"It would be incorrect to state that some beliefs are negative. What would be appropriate is to understand that some beliefs are supportive, and some of them are non-supportive. While supportive beliefs build us, non-supportive beliefs tear us down. Supportive beliefs make us feel confident about ourselves and our actions. They help us in accomplishing our aspirations. Supportive beliefs help us stay focused on the possibilities and not just the current circumstances."

Examples of supportive beliefs

- *This may be difficult, but it is not impossible.*
- *I may have made a mistake, but I have learned from it.*
- *Even if I fail this time, I will succeed the next time.*
- *Even if my circumstance bends me, it cannot break me.*
- *My current bad situation will not last forever.*

"Supportive beliefs like these empower us to become better versions of ourselves. When supportive beliefs drive us, we hardly give in to fear or let some passing situation break us."

"Tell us more about non-supportive beliefs, Master."

"Non-supportive beliefs, on the other hand, can dent your confidence and your success. Non-supportive beliefs always put you down instead of encouraging you. They discourage you from taking any action and give you reasons as to why you shouldn't take action or can't take action. As a way of tearing down your confidence, these beliefs will always tell you that you are not good enough, and you lack the ability to succeed. Non-supportive beliefs will find infinite reasons to tell you why you cannot achieve your aspirations. Non-supportive beliefs induce fear and promote the fear of failure."

Examples of non-supportive beliefs

- *No one in my family has ever been great/been an entrepreneur/a sportsman, etc.*
- *I am too old/too young.*
- *Everyone else failed, so I might fail too.*

❖ *Something is better than nothing.*

❖ *I can't be better; I'm not good enough.*

Master continued, "Non-supportive beliefs create friction in your journey. They slow you down and keep you from achieving your aspirations. When non-supportive beliefs drive your life, you fail even before you begin."

Master then asked everyone, "Do you know who is the biggest roadblock in your success?"

"Is it our own self, Master?" I asked.

"You are right, Joy. We can be whatever we want to be; we can do anything that we want to do, but there is only one thing that stops us—it is our own non-supportive beliefs. That's why it is said that the biggest roadblock to our success is our own self and no one else."

"What else can non-supportive beliefs do to us?"

"We cannot expect to win a battle that we do not even fight. Many of our non-supportive beliefs are the reason why we accept defeat even before fighting the battle. One of the vital aspects of human nature is to guard the beliefs we have, whether they are supportive or non-supportive. A lot of times, these beliefs become our survival instincts. We do not even challenge them and end up living a mediocre life.

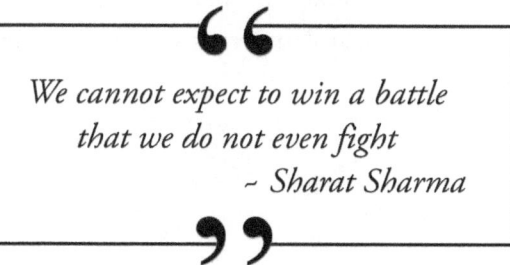

> *We cannot expect to win a battle that we do not even fight*
> *- Sharat Sharma*

Here is an example. Have you ever seen a 6-8-ton elephant kept captive with a small chain or rope? Have you wondered how a small chain or rope enslaves an elephant of that size? A baby elephant, which is manageable in size and strength, is kept captive with a small chain by its master. One end of the chain is fastened to its leg and the other to a tree. Initially, the baby elephant makes attempts to escape, but then it learns that it does not have enough strength to break the chain, so it submits to its master. Soon the baby elephant grows into a massive elephant. As it grows, the belief that it is impossible to break free from the chain also grows. The massive elephant now believes that even if it tries, it will not succeed. So, it chooses to remain captive under the master. It fails to recognize that the tiny chain can be broken easily now. It does not exercise a choice to fight harder. It is no more a captive of its master, but it has succumbed to its own beliefs. The massive elephant has learned to feel helpless.

You can aspire to write the next bestseller, earn the money that you want, or start the next big business, which you have always wanted to. But what holds you back are the non-supportive beliefs. You may make a few attempts, but when your attempts fail, you teach yourself to feel helpless. This helplessness often shows up in the form of excuses and complaints. Every time you find yourself complaining or giving excuses, take a pause, and validate the beliefs that are driving you to give those excuses and complaints."

"So, how does one identify their non-supportive beliefs?" someone asked.

"Your non-supportive beliefs are usually the voice between your ears. They are the excuses and complaints that you often hear from yourself. Let me explain in detail."

***

Steps to identify your non-supportive beliefs

#1: Think, think of an area in your life where you currently face challenges, or where you are unable to make enough progress. For example: In the area of health, your aspiration is to achieve the ideal BMI for your age, but you find it challenging.

#2: Ask yourself this question: *Why can't I achieve my ideal BMI?*

#3: Capture your response in the following syntax.

>I cannot << ... >> because << ... >>

You may answer: *I cannot achieve my ideal BMI because I am genetically this way (or) I cannot achieve my ideal BMI because I have tried everything and nothing seems to work.*

If you break the above sentences, it has the following syntax:

>I cannot << Activity >> because << Belief >>

This syntax is the easiest way to identify some of the non-supportive beliefs that hold you back. Once you identify all the non-supportive beliefs, it is time for you to work on challenging these beliefs.

For example: Let's say your aspiration is to increase your sales by 20%. Your response to 'Why am I unable to achieve 20% sales growth?' might be 'I cannot increase my sales by 20% because I am not a big brand yet' or 'I cannot increase my sales by 20% because the territory that I serve does not have enough customers.'

The above example gives you the list of beliefs.

#4: Examine the non-supportive belief.

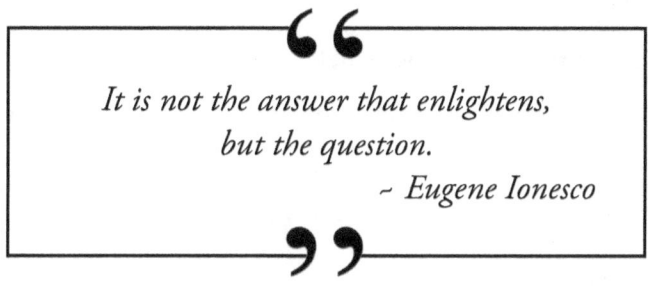

It is not the answer that enlightens, but the question.
~ Eugene Ionesco

Examining our beliefs is the key to expanding the possibilities that life has in store for us. This can be done by questioning them to know whether they are real or imaginary. Byron Katie's four-step framework known as 'The Work' has four powerful questions that you can ask to challenge and rework your beliefs.

Question 1: Is it true?

Question 2: Do you know *for certain* that it is *absolutely* true? Or are there other ways/alternatives to look at it?

Question 3: How do you feel or respond when you consider the belief to be true? How do you treat both the event and yourself?

- Does the thought bring peace or stress in your life?
- What images do you see—in the past and the future?
- What physical sensations arise as you think and witness the thought in images?
- What emotions arise when you believe that thought?
- Does any obsession or addiction appear when you believe that thought? (Do you act out using any of the following: alcohol, drugs, credit cards, food, sex, television, and computers?)
- How do you treat people in this situation when you believe the thought?
- How do you treat yourself?

Question 4: Who would you be without these limiting beliefs?

Put yourself back in the situation, but this time without the belief. How would your experience change? How would you feel this time? What actions will you take?

#5: Empower yourself with new beliefs.

What new supportive beliefs would you want to integrate into your life?

#6: Convert the new beliefs into actions.

***

Steps to identify your non-supportive beliefs

#1: Think of an area in your life where you currently face challenges, or where you are unable to make enough progress.

#2: Ask yourself this question: Why am I not able to make progress?

#3: Capture your response in the following syntax.
I cannot << ... >> because << ... >>

#4: Examine the non-supportive belief.

#5: Empower yourself with new beliefs.

#6: Convert the new beliefs into actions.

I asked Master, "How long should we challenge the non-supportive beliefs?"

Master said, "Joy, This is a constant continuous effort. If you do not challenge, you will end up living with these non-supportive beliefs. Living with these non-supportive beliefs is much easier than challenging them. Living with these non-supportive beliefs takes no effort because all you have to do is – nothing. Challenging, on the other hand, takes effort. Non-supportive beliefs keep you stuck while challenging it helps you learn and grow.

Imagine you are blindfolded. You are not sure if your next step will lead you up the stairs or down a pit, or worse, lead you to crash into a brick wall. But unless you challenge, you won't learn; remember, failure gives you more lessons than staying stuck and doing nothing. You have to challenge the non-supportive beliefs and learn from them; only then will you expand your beliefs.

Joy, begin by challenging the beliefs that are holding you back, the ones that made you believe that things are impossible. Remember, making an effort is what counts. You will always find excuses to say why you cannot do anything. Instead of hanging on to the excuses, build the beliefs that support your aspirations. Replace your non-supportive limiting beliefs with supportive beliefs of possibilities. Once you are clear about your aspirations and have built the right kind of beliefs, nothing can stop you."

"Thanks, Master. This is indeed very helpful."

"Here is another tool that you can use to challenge your beliefs on a regular basis. This model was adapted by Martin Seligman from Albert Ellis' Model. It is called the ABCDE model."

***

A stands for **adversity** (a situation that triggers an emotional response).

B is for the **beliefs** you automatically have about an event/a situation.

C is for the usual **consequences** of the belief (the way you feel or behave).

D is for the **disputation** of your routine belief, using facts and logic.

E is for the **energization** that occurs when you dispute a non-supportive belief successfully.

This simply means you have to pay attention to how you feel. For instance, do you feel lighter or more energized?

Example:

Adversity: You gave a presentation. You didn't use your allocated time, and you stumbled in a few places.

Belief: Your response to the adversity can be – I am really bad at public speaking. I always make a mess of it. I ought not to do it again because I will be bad at it. My boss may think that I am not cut out for the job.

Consequences: You turn down appointments to speak, and therefore miss opportunities that let you influence more people.

Disputation: I haven't had much experience in giving presentations. That was only my third time. The head of the department spoke for less time as well, and no one bothered about it. A number of people asked me questions, and they were interested in what I was saying. Some even said they liked my slides, and many said positive things. I might not have been that fluent, but I was okay. If I can conquer my nerves, I should be better next time.

You may consider the following questions to dispute your irrational thoughts.

1. **What is the evidence?**
   + What evidence do I have to support my thoughts?
   + What evidence do I have against them?
2. **What alternative views are there?**
   + How would an outsider view this situation?
   + How would I have viewed it before I got anxiety/depression?
   + How much more likely are the new alternatives?
3. **How much does thinking this way cost me?**
   + Does it help me or stop me from getting what I want? How?
   + What might be the outcome of looking at things in a healthier way?

4. **Is my thinking realistic? (review the common thinking errors)**
    + Am I thinking in all-or-nothing terms?
    + Am I condemning myself as a total person based on a single event?
    + Am I concentrating on my weaknesses and forgetting my strengths?
    + Am I blaming myself for something that is not my fault?
    + Am I taking something personally that has little or nothing to do with me?
    + Am I expecting myself to be perfect?
    + Am I using double standards? How would I view my best friend in this situation?
    + Am I paying attention only to the bad side of things?
    + Am I overestimating the chances of a disaster?
    + Am I exaggerating the importance of events?
    + Am I doing 'should, must, and ought' instead of accepting and dealing with situations as they are?
    + Am I assuming I can do nothing to change my situation?
    + Am I predicting the future negatively instead of experimenting with it or being excited about it?
5. **What action can I take?**
    + What can I do to change my situation?
    + Am I overlooking solutions to problems on the assumption that they won't work?
    + What can I do to test the alternative views I have arrived at?

Energization

As you dispute the beliefs, you will probably say, "I feel positive, and I am willing to take up the next presentation. I will act on the feedback that I gathered this time."

ABCDE Exercise

Adversity – Think of an event/situation that triggers an emotional response
_____
_____

Beliefs – List down your auto response to such events/ situation.
_____
_____

Consequences – List down the consequences of holding on to the beliefs
_____
_____

Disputation – Dispute the belief that you are holding on to using facts and logic.
_____
_____

Energization – How energized do you feel after disputing non-supportive beliefs successfully.
_____
_____

These were powerful tools that Master had shared. Everyone was happy learning about these tools. After this, people started thanking Master, and in a short time, most of them dispersed. I walked closer to Master and said, "This was another great learning, Master."

We then walked into Master's study room and began our conversation.

I asked, "Master, when should we work on our beliefs? Is that part of the invisible code that high achievers follow?"

Master responded with a smile, "You are right, Joy. Once you set your aspirations right, you must work on challenging your beliefs. That is the next step of the code. You must constantly renew your beliefs to know what more is possible. Remember, your beliefs are your boundaries; you must break them often.

I asked, "How about survivors, explorers, and dabblers? Master said, "A lot of times, what holds anyone back is their belief. The truth is, only when you have a strong aspiration, you will have the willingness to challenge your beliefs. While you are working on setting your aspirations, if you identify with the survivor mindset, explorer mindset, or dabbler mindset, you must invest more time in challenging your beliefs. Even achievers must challenge their beliefs because your aspirations will expand as much as you allow your beliefs to expand."

"I understand this now, Master. I realize the fact that everyone must work on themselves first. Mastering the self is a bigger victory than mastering anything else. It does not really matter whether one is a survivor, explorer, dabbler, or an achiever; what matters is constantly challenging the beliefs."

I spent the rest of the day setting my aspirations and challenging my beliefs. With the promise to meet Master the next day, I went back to my room.

Master had told me to meet him near the swimming pool the next day. I wondered why.

Inspiration Corner

Sir Roger Bannister is regarded as the first man to break the four-minute mile barrier – on May 6, 1954. Before his record-breaking feat, no athlete in human history had ever run a mile in four minutes or less. At that time, there was a popular belief that such a feat was physically impossible. Experts at that time said that anyone who attempted to run a mile in four minutes was at risk of certain death from exploded lungs. Of course, many athletes before Bannister had tried breaking the four-minute mile barrier, but they all failed.

Two years before this record-breaking feat, Bannister had finished fourth at the 1952 Olympics, which he considered a relative failure. He spent two months considering giving up running, but instead, he set a new goal for himself, to break the four-minute mile and be the first man to do so. He began intense physical and mental training. According to Bannister, whenever he trained, he was always positive towards achieving the feat. According to experts, certain conditions had to be precise for the feat to be successfully accomplished. The conditions were: perfect weather of 68 degrees Fahrenheit without wind, a particularly hard, dry, clay track, and a huge crowd chanting cheers of encouragement to the runner. However, Bannister broke the barrier in one of the most unfavorable weather conditions. The day was cold, the track was wet, and the crowd was just a few thousand people.

Sir Roger Bannister broke the four-minute mile barrier by running a mile in 3 minutes 59.4 seconds because he refused to give in to the disempowering belief that had controlled athletes for years. Although his record only lasted for 46 days, history will forever show that Roger Bannister was the first man to run a mile in four minutes—all because he refused to believe in a notion that was not only a physical barrier but a psychological one as well.

Nine thoughts to embrace and create empowering beliefs

1 – Thoughts About Your Potential

What lies behind us and what lies before us are small matters compared to what lies within us.

~ Henry Stanley Haskins

2 – Thoughts About Learning

If you are not willing to learn, no one can help you.
If you are determined to learn, no one can stop you.

~ Anonymous

3 – Thoughts About Opportunities

Opportunity often comes disguised in the form of misfortune or temporary defeat.

~ Napoleon Hill

4 – Thoughts About Failure

The only failure is when you say, "I give up."

~ Unknown

5 – Thoughts About Relationships

A great relationship is about two things; first, find out the similarities, second, respect differences.

~ Unknown

6 – Thoughts About Money

Money is only a tool. It will take you wherever you wish, but it will not replace you as the driver.

~ Ayn Rand

7 – Thoughts About Growth

You will either step forward into growth, or you will step back into safety.

~ Abraham Maslow

8 – Thoughts About Fun

Have fun while working hard; that's the perfect recipe to be successful.

~ Unknown

9 – Thoughts About Health

Happiness is the highest form of health.
So, choose happiness over everything else.

~ Dalai Lama

CHAPTER 9

THE 3Cs – THE START, THE PATH & THE WIN

The 3Cs

The next day, I prepared myself to meet Master near the swimming pool. I was worried as I did not have any experience in swimming; in fact, I always feared drowning. I reached the pool and stood next to the pool nervously.

"How have you been, Joy?" enquired Master. "I hope you had a good sleep."

I nodded in agreement.

Master was in the pool, and, as anticipated, he said, "Joy, why don't you jump in the water and swim along?"

"Master, I don't know how to swim, and I have always had a fear of water."

"Have you ever tried learning how to swim?"

"No, I haven't."

"What beliefs are holding you back? Are you willing to challenge these beliefs?"

I never wanted to challenge my beliefs. But then I thought about how we hold on to our beliefs and make them real. How we do not try new things and limit ourselves from living our potential.

I heard Master say, "Joy, you cannot learn to swim just by standing next to the pool and watching other people swim. You must take the first leap of faith and jump in. You must challenge your old beliefs. Jump in."

With a lot of resistance, I somehow managed to jump in. I struggled for a while and wanted to get out of the pool.

Master saw me struggling and said, "Don't fight with the water, Joy. You must start loving it. The more you fight with it, the more struggles you will face. The more you love the process, the easier it will be."

We spent some time in the pool. I think I swallowed a few gallons of water that day. But I was glad that I could at least get rid of my fear. As we came out of the pool, Master said, "I am happy that you are on the right path, Joy. Today, I want to share the third step of the one invisible code with you. This step has 3Cs, and you have already demonstrated one of the Cs."

"You mean during the swimming lesson?"

"Yes, Joy, you have demonstrated the quality of being courageous, which is the first C."

I looked puzzled.

"You jumped into the pool in spite of having doubts and fears, and that's the first quality you need to break through mediocrity and discover your greatness. Courage is your ability to take action in the face of fear and doubts. A lot of times, when you challenge your beliefs, you will have doubts and fears, but then the only choice in the face of fear is to move forward. Every high achiever is aware that they will face challenges when they are on an aspirational journey. They know exercising courage is the only way to fulfill their aspirations. They understand that, in times of adversity and challenge, they can choose fear and stay stuck, or choose courage and move forward. High achievers choose courage and move forward."

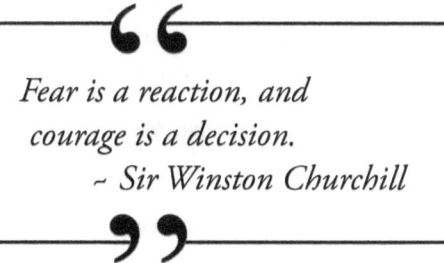

> *Fear is a reaction, and courage is a decision.*
> ~ Sir Winston Churchill

"Master, can one learn to be courageous? I thought it was an innate quality that only a few are blessed to have?"

"Courage is like a muscle; like any muscle, the more you exercise the muscle, the stronger it gets. If you exercise it less, you lose the muscle. So, you must exercise courage to grow courage. You must take smaller risks to prepare yourself to take bigger risks. We often hear that the greatest wealth in the world is found in the graveyard. Do you know why?"

"No, I don't," I said, wondering about the statement Master had made.

"It is because a lot of people die with their precious dreams and ideas still alive in them. These dreams and ideas could have changed the world. Many people never really lived their dreams—not because their dreams were too tough, but because they never had the courage to take the first step. For a moment, imagine if Leonardo Da Vinci had dreams and aspirations but never had the courage to take that first step to do everything that he had done. The world would have missed out on a genius. Elon Musk and Richard Branson do what many others don't. They have the courage to take action regardless of the circumstances, fears, and doubts they have. ISRO (Indian Space Research Organization) exemplifies courage. They attempt the impossible; even though they have failed, they have never stopped themselves from attempting again. Joy, courage doesn't always roar. Sometimes courage is the quiet voice at the end of the day that says, 'I will try again tomorrow.'"

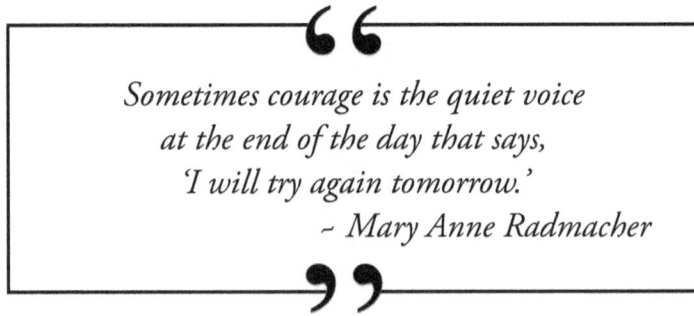

> *Sometimes courage is the quiet voice*
> *at the end of the day that says,*
> *'I will try again tomorrow.'*
> *~ Mary Anne Radmacher*

"What if our actions don't work? What should we do, Master?"

"Joy, the question is not what if things don't work; the question is, what if they do work? You will never know if the action that you take or the decision you make is right or wrong unless you take it. Remember, you cannot learn to swim just by watching others swim."

I smiled.

"Every time you have to take action or make a decision, train yourself to think about all the things that will go right rather than think of all the things that might go wrong. If things go wrong, as they will sometimes, remember you always fail forward. You learn from failure.

This brings me back to your earlier question. Are people courageous, or can courage be learned?

Does a lion need to learn how to rule the jungle? Does a fish need to learn how to swim, or does an eagle need to learn how to fly? We are born courageous and free, but it is our non-supportive beliefs that create fear in us. You must work on the non-supportive beliefs and get rid of the beliefs that make you feel inferior. You must work on being courageous and free. That's what you are meant to be."

"What should be my first step now?"

"Firstly, most people misunderstand courage. To be courageous, you must learn to conquer the irrational fear that stops you and the illogical action that can harm you. The key is not to let yourself be stopped and continue moving towards fulfilling your aspirations."

"Tell me a little more about this, Master."

"Joy, it takes courage to speak; it also takes courage to be silent and listen. It takes courage to stand in the front and lead, and it takes courage to step back and follow. It takes courage to share everything you know, and it takes courage to accept that you do not know and be willing to learn. It takes courage to exercise your strength, and it takes courage to accept your weakness. It takes courage to follow your path, and it takes courage to accept that you are lost and not give up while finding your path. It takes courage to hold on, and it also takes courage to let go. Simply put, it's about knowing when to step forward and take an important action, and

The 'One' Invisible Code

when to step back and introspect. This balance must be practiced in all our endeavors; that's when you will learn to be courageous."

"This one is fantastic, Master. Thank you. Now I understand that being courageous is a virtue that grows when we exercise it. I have never thought of it this way till now. I have always thought of courage from the perspective of being strong and not giving up but not from the perspective of striking a balance."

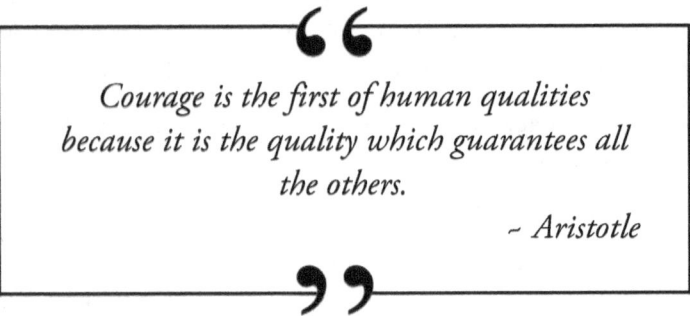

> *Courage is the first of human qualities because it is the quality which guarantees all the others.*
> *~ Aristotle*

"So, what's next, Master?"

Master smiled.

"Joy, it takes courage to get you started, but it is commitment that keeps you going."

Inspirational Story of Kiran Bedi

An inspiration for millions of women today, Kiran Bedi, India's first female IPS officer, is one iconic woman we all truly admire. She has tremendous willpower to fight injustice and stand strong for poor people. She has always made her presence felt with her firm decisions.

She was born on 9th June 1949 in Amritsar, Punjab.

In July 1972, she started police training at the National Academy of Administration, Mussoorie. In the batch of 80 men, she was the only woman.

Kiran Bedi had to face a lot of tough assignments during her initial career, including traffic postings in New Delhi, where she once towed away the car of then Prime Minister, Indira Gandhi, for violating parking rules. After this incident, she was nicknamed as Crane Bedi.

She started a number of reforms during her service period, which brought positive results as well as lots of appreciation from around the world. She initiated yoga, meditation classes, sports, and art groups in jails, which brought about mutual understanding among the jail inmates and police personnel.

Acts of Courage

In the '90s, she was transferred to Tihar Jail, known as the most notorious jail in India. She alone transformed the jail into a peace-loving ashram by introducing literacy and meditation programs. This act of courage fetched her the Magsaysay Award and a memorable place in the history of Indian Police.

- Kiran Bedi single-handedly managed the Punjab separatist movement and fought against the sword-carrying Sikh militants.
- Her courage and achievements have a great influence on women and the younger generation of India. Her speeches have and continue to inspire everyone.

Commitment

Master continued, "When your aspirations are backed by strong belief, courage, and commitment to continue the journey, you are ready to tap into your full potential and turn every aspiration into results."

> *Commitment is that turning point in your life when you seize the moment and convert it into an opportunity to alter your destiny.*
> *~ Denis Waitley*

"Joy, there are many who start working on their aspirations, but only a few continue the pursuit till the end. To continue the pursuit, one must have commitment."

I nodded in acknowledgment of the point that Master had shared.

"Commitment is a virtue of the brave. It happens when you are ready to go all-in and are unwilling to surrender; that's when your aspirations turn into results. Joy, dreaming is easy; getting started on your dreams is the tough step. But believing and giving everything you have is tougher and perhaps rare too. That's the next important thing that you need to reach the next level of success in your journey."

"Keeping the commitment is a bit of a challenge for many, Master."

"Joy, most people just hope. But they don't commit. Commitment is not about hope. When you hope, you don't try enough; when you don't try hard, you rely on miracles. Commitment is about being true to who you are and honoring every word that you speak. It is about trusting the path that you have chosen and following it until the end. Most people, somewhere along their path, start to lose focus on their aspirations. The moment they are hit with a challenge, they give up on their commitment. They go back on their words not because the challenge is too hard but because they never believe what they can achieve if they stay committed."

"Master, it is not intentional, but I do miss out on my commitments."

"Joy, a lot of times, you find yourself longing to start a major project, and when you eventually find the courage to start, you lose interest along the way and end up with another unfinished project. For some people, finding the courage to start something is hard, while for others, the commitment to see it through, till the end, is what they lack.

When it comes to commitment, the only thing that works is the mantra 'do whatever it takes'. Yes, you must do whatever it takes to keep your commitments. Your commitment is like your signature; you are identified by it. When you don't keep your commitments, it kills your self-image and sabotages your confidence. Joy, this means you must do whatever it takes to live up to your commitments."

> ❝
> *Your commitment is like your signature; you are identified by it.*
> ~ Sharat Sharma
> ❞

Commitments you must keep

1. Commitment to be optimistic
2. Commitment to stay focused
3. Commitment to keep your word
4. Commitment to take decisions
5. Commitment to invest wisely
6. Commitment to nurture relationships
7. Commitment to learn
8. Commitment to explore the next level

"When you do whatever it takes, it builds your credibility, and people know you for keeping commitments. It adds to your impact and influence."

Inspiration Corner

I am yet to meet a single person who has tasted the famous Kentucky Fried Chicken (KFC) and has not loved it. They may be out there somewhere, but I just haven't met them. And it is all thanks to Colonel Harland Sanders' commitment to his passion. After getting fired so many times from a number of jobs, he decided to start a chicken cooking business in 1930, at a Shell service station he owned. This was during the Great Depression. Although the gas station had no restaurant, he decided to serve meals in his personal living quarters, which was attached to the service station. He spent about 10 years perfecting his pressure fryer method of cooking his soon-to-be-famous recipe for fried chicken.

However, during the 1950s, after a major highway took away his business, he was forced to shut down, but he remained committed to his dream and passion for preparing fried chicken. His commitment led him to look for restaurants to franchise his secret recipe, and he was willing to accept a nickel for every piece of chicken sold. He got rejected more than a thousand times. He would often sleep in his car while driving around. His commitment finally paid off, and he franchised his secret recipe to the operator of one of the largest restaurants in South Salt Lake, Utah. His recipe became famous in the United

States, Canada, and the UK. Today, you get to enjoy the finger-licking goodness of KFC because of one man's commitment to his aspiration.

"Joy, making and keeping commitments are driven by your mindset. An achiever understands that first you make commitments, and then your commitments make you."

"So, I need to work on my mindset first."

"You are right, Joy. You can also start small and grow one step at a time. It's like climbing the mountain, one step at a time. As you begin to develop the habit of making and keeping commitments, your self-image and confidence improves. You are then ready to make bigger commitments. You should gradually step up your commitment and take on bigger projects.

Making and fulfilling smaller commitments to conquer bigger ones sounds like a great idea. When your aspirations are clear, your beliefs are strong; you are courageous enough to take that first step and are fully committed, you are one step closer to tap into your potential and fulfill your aspirations."

"What's the next C, Master?" I asked with curiosity.

"Joy, courage gets you started, commitment keeps you going, but it is the 3rd C that takes you to the next level of success."

"What is that, Master?"

"Joy, everything that I have told you so far is a part of your inner world. Your aspirations, beliefs, courage, and commitment are all invisible. To bridge the invisible and visible, to make the inner world match the outer results, you need the 3rd C, which is competence. Courage gets you started, commitment keeps you going, and competence makes sure that you win.

Competence is one's ability, skills, and knowledge (ASK) to perform a certain task. A lot of times, you might have great aspirations, positive beliefs, the courage to take the first step, and commitment to stay on track, but what you might be lacking is the competence to perform the task at an optimum level."

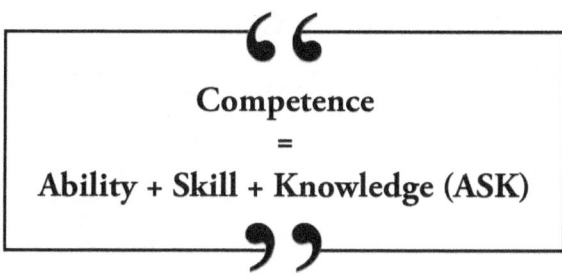

"Imagine for a moment, Joy. You jump into the battlefield, aspiring to win. You have the belief, you have the courage to take the first step, and you are committed to winning. Then you realize that you are not competent enough to use the weapons. What will happen to you?"

"I will not only lose, but I will also be killed!"

Master replied with a smile, "True Joy, you run the risk of killing yourself. That's exactly why developing competence to win is the key to your success. It is one thing to aspire and another thing to act, but it is a whole different thing to have the competence to win.

About a year ago, I met a young man who played the guitar very well. Whenever he played, people were awestruck by his talent. I once asked him how he managed to play the tunes that got everyone so involved. He said, 'I practiced for 30 minutes every day since the age of seven.' He was 23 when I met him.

When you put all these together, you will discover that he has been practicing for 1, 75,200 minutes! That's the power of consistent practice. The secret is simple: your practice improves your competence."

"How do I identify the competency gap?"

Bridging The Competency Gap

1) List down the competencies that you need to fulfill your aspirations.
2) Evaluate your current levels of competence
3) Identify the required level of competence
4) Identify the gap between the current and required level of competence.
5) List down the things that you must do consistently to improve your competence.

"Every successful individual we celebrate today recognizes that competence is the key to achieve massive results. All of them credit their success to the competence developed through practice. Musicians, sportsmen, actors, and many others agree that the world changes rapidly, and to stay relevant and reach their next level of success, they must constantly work on improving their competence."

Inspiration Corner

Dr. K. Anders Ericsson, a Swedish psychologist, says deliberate practice, not inherited talent, determines success.

Take Michael Jordan, one of the best athletes the world has seen. From him, you learn that talent is necessary, but talent alone won't take you to the top of world-class contenders. To rise to the top, you've got to practice, practice, practice, and stick to a well-thought-out plan. Even with his talents, which included exceptional physical strength and height, Michael Jordan was ultra-determined and practiced vigorously every day for most of his professional career.

The famous Michael Jackson was a prodigy when it came to vocals. But he had to become competent in his dance moves and choreography in order to be unique. Michael Jackson was popularly known as the 'king of pop' due to his style of music and unique dance moves. He understood how important competence was to be successful. That was why he committed a lot of time to rehearse his dance routines and was sometimes reported to have sustained injuries during rehearsals. His commitment to becoming competent always yielded results, as he is loved even today by many, even after his death.

Master continued, "The fact is, life will present you with opportunities at some point or the other, but if you are not competent, it is hard to take advantage of these opportunities. When you are competent, you will not only take advantage of the opportunities but also create opportunities. Whatever your aspirations are, you need the competence to accomplish them."

"How long does this journey of improving competence last?"

"Joy, leaders are learners, and learners are leaders! We never stop learning. Learning and improving your competence happens from the womb to the tomb. You must always strive to improve your knowledge, learn a new skill, and challenge your abilities. To understand this, you must understand the levels of competence that Dreyfus and Dreyfus proposed."

Levels of competence

Novice: Rule-based behavior, strongly limited, and inflexible

Experienced beginner: Incorporates aspects of the situation

Practitioner: Acts consciously from long-term goals and plans

Knowledgeable practitioner: Sees the situation as a whole and acts from personal conviction

Expert: Has an intuitive understanding of the situation and zooms in on the central aspects

The process of competency development is a lifelong series of doing and reflecting.

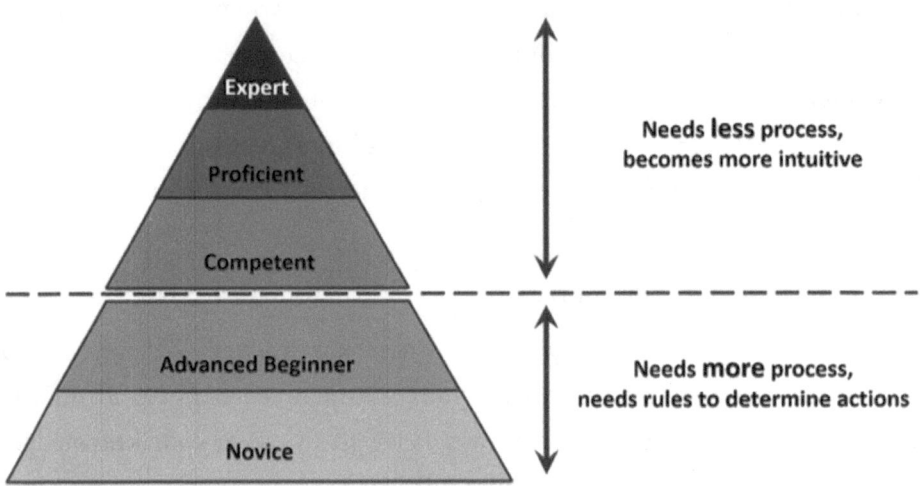

Master explained the levels, "The key to growing from a novice to an expert is practice. Every bigger aspiration will require you to have a new level of competence. So, you must continue to evaluate, improve, and practice."

"What are some of the ways through which I can improve my ability, skills, and knowledge? What are the things that I should practice?" I asked.

"That's a great question! I would like to suggest a few ways."

***

Things to practice to improve competence

1) **Read**: One of the greatest sources for improving your competence is books. Books inspire you and teach you life skills. They give you access to the minds of people who have achieved mastery in their space of work. Do read biographies of great leaders; they help you understand the beliefs of great leaders and how they changed the world.

2) **Training**: Identify the gap between where you are and where you want to be on the specific skills you need to fulfill your aspirations. Create a clear roadmap to bridge the gap by investing in training. The harder you train, the more you gain.

3) **Join masterminds**: Masterminds are groups of people who come together for mutual growth and improvement. You must join masterminds that are aligned to your aspirations and those that help you improve your competence.

4) **Hire a coach**: A lot of times, we are blindsided by our wisdom and miss seeing our demons. A coach can help you find these blind spots and design a development plan to improve.

***

"These are amazing, Master!"

As we progressed, each step of the one invisible code made me feel more confident. I admitted this to Master and expressed my delight in learning the powerful and simple invisible code that he had shared.

"So, these are the 3Cs that you need. We now have one last step to complete the one invisible code, Joy. Are you excited to learn about the last step?"

We decided to meet the next day to discuss the last step of the invisible code.

Bridging The Competency Gap

1) List down the competencies that you need to fulfill your aspirations.
   _____
   _____

2) Evaluate your current levels of competence
   _____
   _____

3) Identify the required level of competence
   _____
   _____

4) Identify the gap between the current and required level of competence.
   _____
   _____

5) List down the things that you must do consistently to improve your competence.
   _____
   _____

You'll never change your life until you change something you do daily. The secret of your success or happiness is found in your daily routine.
  ~ John C. Maxwell

CHAPTER 10

THE 5DS – THE FREEDOM

Discipline

The next day

I was happy that I would be learning the final piece of the invisible code today. This was the final piece of the puzzle. I was ready for the day. I quickly gathered all my notes and went to meet Master.

"Joy, you are just one step away from discovering the one invisible code."

"I am eager and looking forward to it, Master."

"The final step of the one invisible code is discipline."

I instantly said, "I hate discipline."

Master smiled and said, "Joy, most people hate discipline. When the discipline is set based on strong aspirations, your results accelerate. Discipline is like a set of rituals, rules, and protocols that you must follow every day to stay on track and achieve every result you aspire. Most people have routines, but people who are high achievers have rituals. Rituals are consciously designed by you, whereas routine is the default behavior.

When you are aspirational, life is highly demanding and also fulfilling. If you don't consciously design your rituals, you will get carried away by other demanding distractions. That's why you must be disciplined and set rituals. I am reminded of a famous saying, 'Discipline sets you free'."

"How can discipline set me free, Master?"

"If you want the freedom to do the things that you want to do, you need more time. The only way to find more time is to be disciplined with how you use your time. If you want more money, you must be disciplined with your spending; you must invest wisely. If you want to be free from diseases, you must be disciplined in keeping your mental, emotional, and physical wellbeing intact. Being disciplined can give you more of what you want so that you are not chained by constraints."

"Got it, Master!"

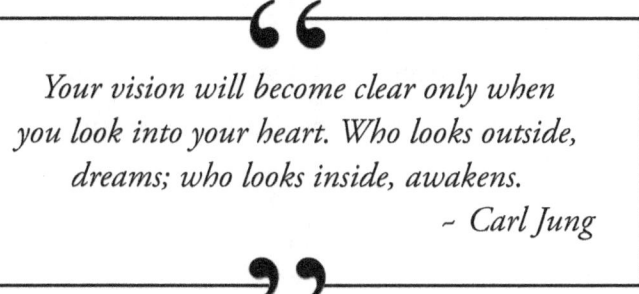

> *Your vision will become clear only when you look into your heart. Who looks outside, dreams; who looks inside, awakens.*
> *~ Carl Jung*

"Discipline also builds your mindset. Your everyday discipline includes the habits that you build to support your aspirations and refine your mindset. The more you work on your discipline, the more you shape your mindset. Your discipline is a set of non-negotiable activities that make you achieve more out of less time. It sets you on an accelerated trajectory of results. Initially, you build discipline consciously. Then your discipline builds you. Discipline brings stability, structure, and control in our lives."

Five reasons that will inspire you to be disciplined

- ❖ Being disciplined can help you craft the future you want.
- ❖ It keeps you on track so that you make progress.
- ❖ It minimizes resistance and creates flow.
- ❖ It makes you strong—financially, emotionally, and physically.
- ❖ It also makes you experience happiness and fulfillment.

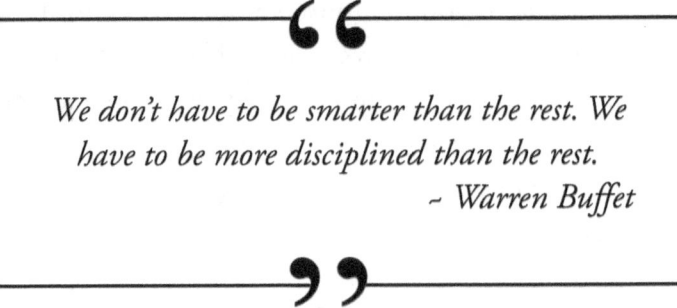

We don't have to be smarter than the rest. We have to be more disciplined than the rest.
~ Warren Buffet

"What are the top disciplines that you recommend, Master?"

"I recommend that you follow the five disciplines that I have highlighted in this book."

Master then took out a book and gave it to me. "I use this book each day, and this is a gift from me to you. As you head back to start a new life, the next level productivity planner will come in handy. I have highlighted all the five disciplines. Let me explain all the five everyday disciplines and why you must follow them."

Five disciplines to reach your next level of success

#1 Discipline of being grateful

We spoke about gratitude while setting aspirations. It is great to have it as an everyday ritual.

Being grateful makes you more graceful. Gratitude opens your heart to endless possibilities and lets you experience the flow of life. Noticing simple pleasures and acknowledging them makes you happier and more resilient. It shifts your focus from what life lacks to the abundance that is already present. Being grateful also strengthens your relationship with the self and others; it improves health and reduces stress.

Gratitude anchors you to be in the present moment. It helps you realize that everything is fine just the way it is. It helps us stop fighting and resist controlling, striving, and chasing happiness, and urges us to accept the flow. You must start your day with gratitude. As a result, you experience not just tremendous joy, but you also become a part of the flow. Instead of being reactive, you set a proactive approach to accomplish a lot more each day.

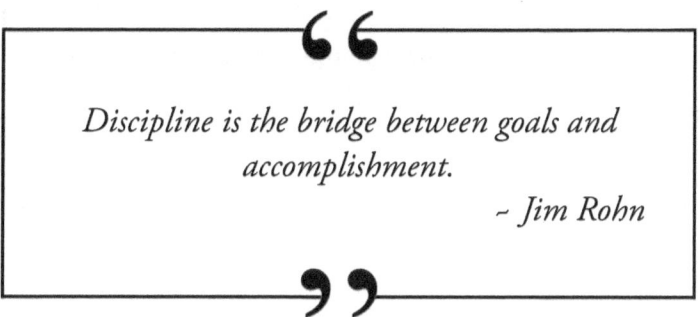

Discipline is the bridge between goals and accomplishment.
~ Jim Rohn

#2 Discipline of Planning

Proper planning prevents poor performance.

Planning helps you design the day, week, or even month. It is highly unlikely that you can plan and execute in parallel, especially when you are working on massive and critical projects. So, you must first plan. Unfortunately, planning is highly underrated. Planning is like creating a blueprint much before you lay the foundation to the beautiful castle that you wish to build. The fact is, if the blueprint is clear, the result is easier and quicker.

There is a famous saying: Failing to plan is planning to fail. Hence, you need to plan every day.

#3 Discipline of measuring

If planning helps you design the blueprint, then measuring helps you stay on course with the plan. Marrying clear planning and measuring helps you accelerate the results. Measuring also indicates when to shift the momentum of your game. A disciplined effort to measure your efforts helps you make course correction, if necessary. You must discipline yourself to do better than you did yesterday. As you make your daily plans and measure your progress, your progress becomes predictable.

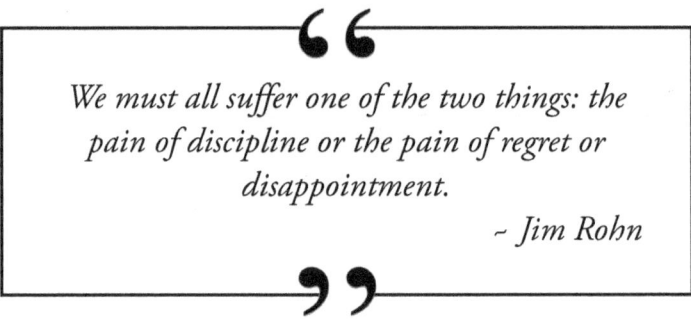

> *We must all suffer one of the two things: the pain of discipline or the pain of regret or disappointment.*
> ~ Jim Rohn

#4 Discipline of Focus

Where focus goes, energy flows! In the world that is screaming for attention, your focus is your biggest asset. It helps you gain control of your results. Our lives are a result of our focus, and when you constantly focus on what truly matters, life starts to present possibilities. For you to stay focused, you must constantly be aware of the things that will take your focus off. You need to know what distractions need to be eliminated. Disciplining yourself to focus is not going to be easy, but if you are determined and patient, you will notice that the results are worth the effort.

To discipline your focus, practice the strategy of 'time block'. It is the most powerful tool when you want to get more work done and stay highly productive. Time blocking is when you set aside a block of time and fill it with the most important tasks at hand. You must practice single-minded focus during this time block. You must get rid of all distractions during this block. Do not multitask, and focus only on getting one thing done. When you practice this strategy, you learn to get more done in less time.

#5 Discipline of Learning

Learning is the treasure that will follow its owner everywhere. Learners are earners. When we love to remain as students of our own life, growth and success are inevitable. Learning is and should be an important part of your daily discipline. The fact about our everyday life is that it never stops teaching us great lessons.

There are two types of learning: dedicated learning through books, masterminds, and training sessions to improve your competence, and the other one is learning from everyday life. Everyday lessons are usually found in the obstacles you face. Be aware and learn from these obstacles. Let it be the source of your greatest learning.

When you use the next level productivity planner, you will get an opportunity to gather your learning each day. Let your learning inspire you to be more, do more, and have more.

Note: The five disciplines mentioned here are available in the form of a planner in *The Next Level Productivity Planner*. To know more about this planner, you can visit my website www.sharatsharma.in

Here is how you plan your everyday disciplines. Master took over, "Joy, you have the code that has helped many."

Sample of the Daily Planner provided in the next page.

PLAN

THE NEXT LEVEL
DAILY PLANNER
____/____/20____

"The best way to predict the future is to create it."
– Abraham Lincoln

GRATITUDE

My gratitude list : Today I am grateful of
1. _____
2. _____
3. _____
4. _____
5. _____

My message to self : _____

PLANNING

Planning : What are my 5 tasks for today   Priority
1. _____   L ○ ○ ○ ○ ○ H
2. _____   L ○ ○ ○ ○ ○ H
3. _____   L ○ ○ ○ ○ ○ H
4. _____   L ○ ○ ○ ○ ○ H
5. _____   L ○ ○ ○ ○ ○ H

FOCUS

                                          Block Time
My 3 most important tasks for today   Start   End   Total Time
1. _____
2. _____
3. _____

REVIEW

THE NEXT LEVEL
DAILY PLANNER

____/____/20____

"Strive not to be a success, but rather to be of value."
— Albert Einstein

1. My overall progress score of the day

   LOW 1 2 3 4 5 6 7 8 9 10 HIGH

2. My 3-dimensional score of the day

   Mental   L 1 [_____] 10 H
   Emotional L 1 [_____] 10 H
   Physical L 1 [_____] 10 H

3. My overall productivity of the day

   LOW 1 2 3 4 5 6 7 8 9 10 HIGH

4. My top 3 learnings of the day

1. _____
2. _____
3. _____

MEASURE

LEARNING

DISCIPLINES

| Gratitude | Planning | Focus | Measure | Learning |

ADDITIONAL NOTES FOR THE DAY

....
....
....
....

The 'One' Invisible Code

> The One Invisible Code
> =
> Aspirations +
> Beliefs +
> Courage, Commitment, Competence +
> 5 Disciplines

Setting Aspirations

G.A.P.P

Challenging Beliefs

Identifying Non-Supportive Beliefs Challenging Beliefs using "The Work" ABCDE Methods

5 Disciplines

1. Gratitude
2. Planning
3. Measuring
4. Focus
5. Learning

3 Cs

1. Courage – Acting in spite of doubts & fears
2. Commitment – Doing what you say and saying what you do
3. Competence - Novice to Expert

"Joy, this code with the right mindset helps you break through all the mediocre results and takes you to the next level of personal and professional success."

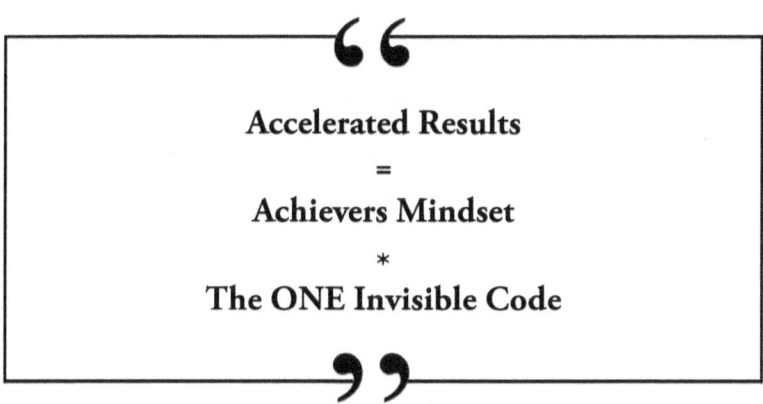

> **Accelerated Results**
>
> =
>
> **Achievers Mindset**
>
> *
>
> **The ONE Invisible Code**

This was the greatest gift that Master gave me that day. Over the next few days, I stayed with Master and designed my life ahead. Here are the things that I did:

1) I first set my aspirations using the GAPP Method
2) I worked on my beliefs to build the mindset of an achiever.
3) I committed to take action towards fulfilling my aspirations. I also did an analysis of my competence
4) I set the five disciplines that Master recommended me to follow

I left Master to pursue these aspirations, deciding to share this wisdom with everyone that I meet in my life.

The journey which started with chaos in my mind turned out to be the most important journey of my life. That's probably the reason why it is said, 'In all chaos there is a cosmos, in all disorder a secret order.' I found my order. I found The One Invisible Code.

> *In all chaos there is a cosmos, in all disorder a secret order.*
>
> – *Carl Jung*

The Way Forward

It's been 10 years since I began implementing the One Invisible Code in various aspects of my life. I have a grown professionally as well as personally using this code. Not only that, I have coached, trained, and mentored several individuals and organizations to use the One Invisible Code. The code has helped individuals find the right job, build great relationships, fulfill aspirations, grow their business, and also multiply their income.

Many entrepreneurs have been able to find how their mindset stopped them from scaling up. Many organizations and leadership teams implemented the One Invisible Code to align their teams towards the right aspirations, shift their beliefs, and build a culture of accountability and ownership.

In the next few pages, there are a few case studies that showcase how the lessons from this book have helped organizations break through mediocrity and rise to their next level of success.

Case Study #1: Change Management

On the path to being the best, you will always face challenges and these challenges will demand you to change. This is a known fact. In spite of knowing this fact, most often, every change is met with resistance.

Many a times, resistance towards change keeps showing up. The resistance can usually be seen in the form of non-cooperation, blame games, or withdrawal from work. This has a huge invisible impact on people, business, and eventually, the bottom line of the company.

This was the case with one of the units of a large pharmaceutical company. The organization was going through several changes. Though everything looked normal on the surface, there were several unsettled emotions within the organization. The human resource team noticed a lot of resistance among a few senior leaders. The speed at which the organization was changing, it could not afford to have this issue unaddressed.

After doing an analysis of the situation, I noticed that most of the teams were in the Orbit of Mediocrity. I realized the need for the teams to understand the Orbit of Mastery. I worked with the teams to expand their awareness and then examined how lack of awareness was causing a lot of resistance within them. We then introspected on what are the things they must accept and take responsibility for. We then designed an action plan to bring changes.

After the successful implementation of the framework, the team's resistance vanished. This gave way to implementing various changes in the organization at the required speed and agility.

Case study #2: Aspiring to be #1

One of the leading organizations in the space of entertainment wanted to reach the #1 spot and be the market leader. The leader's aspiration was to reach the #1 spot within a year. However, the members of the team felt otherwise.

The teams did not have a compelling reason to work towards being #1. The team members were given goals, but they always fell short of achieving them.

It was clearly a case where the team members were not aligned with their leader's aspirations. Also, individuals had different mindsets and it was a must for the teams to shift their mindsets and follow the One Invisible Code to accelerate their results.

I worked with the teams to first shift their mindsets and turn them into achievers. Then I introduced the One Invisible Code to accelerate their results.

During the interactions with the team, I created an emotionally-driven and compelling aspiration. They were asked why they should be the market leaders. We then aligned the individual's professional aspiration with the organization's aspiration. The most important element was to work on building the belief that it was possible. After doing a competency gap study, we created a step-by-step growth roadmap for the team. We designed specific disciplines which could help them reach their aspiration of being #1.

Last year, the organization was awarded the #1 spot and was recognized as the market leader. The organization recognized that the One Invisible Code helped them win this recognition.

Case Study #3: Lost Aspirations

Rahul, an IT professional, was stuck in a job that was not very fulfilling. He was merely surviving in a job, reacting to various escalations most of the time. He was frustrated and wanted to find a job which could be fulfilling.

He was unclear about what he wanted to accomplish and how he could take the path that would give him fulfillment. Every time he set goals and did not achieve them, he closed himself and fought his battles alone.

During our coaching session, the first thing that we worked on was shifting his mindset from being a survivor to an achiever. The moment he shifted his mindset, a lot of aspects in his life started changing. He found an ideal life partner first. He later used the One Invisible Code to identify his real aspirations. Having found his aspiration, he pursued it relentlessly. He changed his job and in a year's time got promoted as the Vice-President in his organization. He often said to me, "Thinking like an achiever has been a game changer!"

MY STORY

At the age of 20, I had my first encounter with entrepreneurship. I started a food catering business when I was still pursuing graduation. After a year, I also started a fast-food joint. Being the first entrepreneur in the family, most of the lessons I learned about entrepreneurship came by the virtue of experiencing failure.

After running these businesses for over 3 years, I gave everything up to pursue my career with major corporations. My corporate experience lasted for over 7 years. I worked with 2 major corporations.

The experience of running a catering business and working in major corporations gave me the opportunity to understand people & business deeply.

In the year 2013, I decided to give wings to my dreams and started my full-time entrepreneurial journey.

In the last decade, I have had the opportunity of coaching 100s of organizations including several fortune 500 companies.

My purpose is to inspire every individual I meet to achieve mastery by **maximizing their potential & multiplying their results.**

I offer simplified solutions to complex problems. This makes me the "go-to coach" of several businesses and individuals.

I was awarded as "Young Entrepreneur For Business Excellence" for my contribution in the field of education.

I frequently contribute on platforms like Entrepreneurs.com, People Matters and many other authority websites.

Scan the QR Code to download the GAPP Template,
Belief System Exercises, The 5 Disciplines Exercise, and
a lot more interesting work by the author.

ACKNOWLEDGEMENT

I'm eternally grateful to the two women in my life. My mom, Vidyotam, she gave me life and my wife, Amruta, she added more life into me. They have taught me discipline, love, patience, and so much more. This book would not have existed without their support.

The constant encouragement from my father, my sister, my brother and my other family members has been instrumental in making this book possible.

I am ever indebted to my guru, Shri Ramakant Maharaj, and all my mentors who have constantly blessed me with their wisdom over the years.

Without the experiences and support from my friends, my peers and my team, this book would not be real.

Special thanks to Madhu Babu for creating wonderful pencil sketches and adding more life to this book and the characters.

To all the individuals I have had the opportunity to train and coach, I want to say thank you for being the inspiration.

Thank you, everyone on the publishing team.

BIBLIOGRAPHY

Many of the short inspiring stories mentioned in the book have created a significant impact on me. I am grateful and acknowledge every writer and speakers whose work has inspired me at different points of time in my journey.

Page 18: Anthony Burgess Story

https://inspiringy.blogspot.com/2015/12/if-i-had-just-year-to-live-how-would-i.html

Page 96: Srikanth Bolla Story

https://www.startupstories.in/stories/inspirational-stories/srikanth-bolla-the-inspiring-entrepreneur

Page 92: J K Rowling Story

https://steemit.com/partiko/@ahtasshamkhan/seemit-success-story-pryuafd6

Page 148: Sir Roger Bannister

Source: Unknown

Page 156: Kiran Bedi Story

http://womenpla.net/inspirational-story-of-kiran-bedi-indias-first-ips-officer/

Page 159: KFC

Souce: Unknown

Page 162: Micheal Jordan & Micheal Jokson Story

Souce: Unknown